The Scriptures Jesus Knew

a guide to the Old Testament

I can recommend *The Scriptures Jesus Knew*: for the amount of basic relevant information, presented with order and clarity of language (not technical jargon); for its sound critical stance, ready to criticise the critics; for its wide cultural horizon and openness to different trends and opinions; for the suggestions of further reading.

Luis Alonso Schökel, SJ, professor of Old Testament,
Pontifical Biblical Institute, Rome

This is a book for beginners in the study of the Old Testament. Its aim is to enable those beginners to encounter the Word of God in his incarnation in the text of the Old Testament in such a way that they can and will want to go on with this adventure. Charles Hill sets the Old Testament and its reader firmly within their respective worlds—culturally, historically and in terms of religion. Readers quickly get a taste for the lively interaction they can have with the text. Most importantly, they are given the tools with which to further that interaction. This is a book which respects both the text of the Old Testament and its readers and encourages their acquaintance.

Rev. Howard N. Wallace, professor of Old Testament, United Faculty of
Theology, the University of Melbourne

This fresh and imaginative introduction to the Old Testament provides a solid initiation into textual analysis, critical method, and biblical-theological themes. It both informs and stimulates. It is clearly the work of an experienced and masterly teacher.

Daniel J. Harrington, SJ, Weston School of Theology, Boston, author of
Interpreting the Old Testament

The Scriptures Jesus Knew

a guide to the Old Testament

CHARLES HILL

E.J.DWYER

First published in 1994 by
E.J. Dwyer (Australia) Pty Ltd
3/32–72 Alice Street
Newtown NSW 2042
Australia
Phone: (02) 550 2355
Fax: (02) 519 3218

National Library of Australia
Cataloguing-in-Publication data

Hill, Charles, 1931– .
    The scriptures Jesus knew: a guide to the Old Testament.

    Includes index.
    ISBN 0 85574 365 4.

1. Bible. O.T.—Introductions. 2. Bible. O.T.—Criticism, interpretation, etc.
I. Title.

221.6

Copy-edited by Eric Sidoti
Cover design by Simon Leong
Text design by Katrina Rendell
Typeset in 11/13 pt Bembo by DOCUPRO, Sydney
Printed in Australia by Southwood Press, Marrickville

10 9 8 7 6 5 4 3 2 1
98 97 96 95 94

Distributed in Canada by:
    Meakin and Associates
    Unit 17
    81 Auriga Drive
    NEPEAN, ONT K2E 7Y5
    Ph: (612) 226 4381
    Fax: (613) 226 1687

Distributed in the United States by:
    Morehouse Publishing
    871 Ethan Allen Highway
    RIDGEFIELD CT 06877
    Ph: (203) 431 3927
    Fax: (203) 431 3964

Distributed in Ireland and the U.K. by:
    Columba Book Service
    93 The Rise
    Mount Merrion
    BLACKROCK CO. DUBLIN
    Ph: (01) 283 2954
    Fax: (01) 288 3770

Dedicated to
the Confraternity of Christian Doctrine,
who generously break the bread of the Word to the
needy.

ACKNOWLEDGMENTS

Rabbi Raymond Apple, AM, of the Great Synagogue, Sydney, has been generous in supplying materials on the teaching of TaNaK.

The author is grateful also to Elizabeth Carey, of the CCD, Sydney, for her invaluable assistance with maps and tables in this book.

Permission of CollinsDove, Melbourne, is acknowledged to reproduce the table "Composition of the Old Testament: A timeline of key figures, events, authors" from *Jesus and the Mystery of Christ* by Charles Hill (1993).

Scripture quotations are from the New Revised Standard Version of the Bible, copyright 1989 by the Division of Christian Education of the National Council of the Churches of Christ in the USA. Used by permission. All rights reserved.

The Fathers on the Old Testament Word

Dwelling in (the Old Testament prophets), the Word spoke of himself. He was, in fact, his own herald ahead of time, showing that the Word was due to appear among people . . . Therefore, let us 'see' the Scriptures, because the Word who was to become manifest preached (through them).

Hippolytus of Rome, *Against Noetus* 11–12

This Word was preached in Law and Prophets as coming into the world. In just the same manner as he was preached did he come and manifest himself by becoming a new human being from the virgin and the Holy Spirit.

Hippolytus, *Against Noetus* 17

Having received of his fullness (*Jn* 1.16), the prophets sang of the things that had been received of the fullness, and so the sacred volumes breathe the spirit of fullness, and there is nothing in Prophecy, in the Law, in the Gospel, or in the Apostle which does not come down from the fullness of divine majesty.

Origen, *Homily on Jeremiah* 51.6

The Lord is prophet, the Lord is Word of God, and no prophet prophesies without the Word of God; the Word of God is with the prophets, and the Word of God is prophet. Former times were thought worthy to have people inspired, filled with the Word of God; we have been thought worthy of the Word of God in person as our prophet.

Augustine, *Commentary on John* 24,7

Whoever loves God's letters and has no wish to be ever ignorant knows everything about them and makes a diligent search after every detail.

Augustine, *Sermons* 232,1

In giving you a commentary on the holy Scriptures, we are as it were breaking bread for you. Consume it in your hunger, and let your heart belch forth in an outburst of praise . . . What I provide you with is not my own: what I eat, you eat; what gives you life gives me life. We have a common store in heaven; it is from there, after all, that the Word of God comes.

Augustine, *Sermons* 95,1

CONTENTS

Chapter 14   DIRECTIONS OF FURTHER STUDY

List of maps and tables

INTRODUCTION

This book has a role to play as a go-between, bringing together two persons who might otherwise not meet, to the great detriment of one of you. I refer to yourself as a believer and to the Word in whom you believe; perhaps you have not got to know the Word as fully as you would like and need to. The Word comes to us in many forms; it is his coming in the texts of the Old Testament that is the object of attention here. A go-between drops out of sight once the meeting of the two has taken place to their mutual satisfaction. In this case, once you have come to be familiar and at ease with the Word of God in the many and varied books of the Old Testament, this guide will have achieved its purpose and can be put aside.

Unfortunately, a great number of people, believers though they be, have not had the experience of such a fruitful meeting—they and the Word remain strangers. To them these intriguing books remain closed. They have to depend on the slimmer, less varied and admittedly less puzzling texts in the New Testament, which themselves talk glowingly of "the Scriptures" these believers may never get to know.

That is a great pity, considering the importance the New Testament itself places on them in Christian formation: they are inspired by God, valuable for instructing and for guidance in good living, so that the person who is God's is now ready for anything, equipped for every good work. So says Paul to Timothy (*2 Tim* 3.16–17) in advising him on his Christian and pastoral responsibilities.

THE SCRIPTURES JESUS KNEW

Still more importantly for us, these are the Scriptures Jesus knew and read (he clearly could not turn up the text of Paul and the evangelists!). It was precisely the message they contained to which he summoned people who had lost the way; it was to no new God or new religion he was calling them—just a closer acquaintance with a Word they had long been given. Jesus read them in his habitual Jewish liturgy (remember the synagogue at Nazareth), spoke often of Moses (as spokesman *par excellence* of the Old Testament) or, in another phrase of similar import, of the Law and the prophets. He called religious officials to proper observance of Old Testament teaching, and at least twice (that we are told of) lectured his disciples on a total grasp of these books as a framework for understanding his life and death.

Hence the title of this book, *The Scriptures Jesus Knew*. It is their role in his own formation and his teaching that makes them precious to us his followers and explains the continuing importance the New Testament and early Christian community give to them. To *all* of them, that is—not to just a limited edition that comes out of rabbinic revision well after Jesus' death and the parting of the two communities that were still worshipping and reading together in his lifetime. The present Hebrew Bible does not adequately represent the Jewish Scriptures of Jesus' time when, though Law (better, Torah) and Prophets were already closed collections, the Writings—containing psalms, Wisdom material, apocalyptic and more—were still undetermined. Among them were works later excluded on various grounds by the rabbis for their community after the first Christian century or two but included in the collection of the Christian East and West until the Reformation. (We shall look in detail at this messy matter of *canon* in chapter 3.) We need to know the Scriptures Jesus knew, as all Christians are admitting these ecumenical days.

That is one good reason or two for not simply using *Old Testament* in our title. Another is the clumsy, churchy term *testament*. It's the anglicised form of the Latin *testamentum*, which translates the Greek word for the Hebrew word for *covenant, treaty, alliance*. This itself is but a figure of speech for "relationship", the relationship which God enters into with a chosen people and which is worked out in the record (spoken and then written) we now have.

Involved, isn't it? Who would see all that behind *Old Testament*? We need to, and will, if we are to plumb the meaning of the library it represents. (For these and other shortcomings of the term, see Appendix 1, "What's in a name?")

A MEETING WITH THE WORD

In short, if we want to get to know the Scriptures Jesus knew, we turn to that wider canon of the Old Testament used by all the Christian churches until the Reformation and now once again being read by all. In Jesus himself, whom the Fathers will call *verbum abbreviatum*, God's Word is summed up in one person. But we are anxious also to meet the Word of God in the textual form of the Bible, something that we may have been deprived of. This meeting with the Word, for which the present book serves merely as go-between, is primarily a *theological* exercise, initiated and conducted in *faith*. Our Creed tells us, "He has spoken through the prophets (= inspired composers of the Bible)." We are not reading the Old Testament primarily to learn more about the *religion* of the Jews—it was not composed for that purpose—nor as a *history* of that people, though we will learn something of these and other incidental matters in the course of reading. We get to meet biblical characters *theologizing*—Job struggling to make sense of life's inequities; Second Isaiah urging the exiles to have confidence in a God who can create anew a way through the wilderness and bring them home; The Chronicler giving them a model for life in the restored community against the background of past infidelities; the psalmist praying for life and light—*theologians* all.

That is the Word speaking, to whom we listen in faith. To hear him clearly, incarnate in word and text, we need to attend to those *incarnational factors* like the culture of the ancient near eastern composers, their ways of assembling their material, the passage from spoken word to written text, and the like. A guide to the Old Testament will help the reader to bridge the gap between our time and the biblical composers' in these and other matters; so each chapter, in introducing readings of different types of text, will broach such issues as authorship, composition, literary types, inspiration and biblical truth, interpretation, biblical revelation, biblical criticism. Otherwise, readers could fall into a simplistic, fundamentalist approach, not appreciating the differences between those distant times and customs and ours—just as it is possible to fail to appreciate Jesus as a Jewish male of the first century who was raised and taught in a style different from our own.

So this guide to the Scriptures Jesus knew, while situating them within the history of Israel and the geography and culture of the ancient east, aims to achieve a meeting of the reader with the Word. The *text* of the Old Testament is basic. In guiding the reader through a wide range of those Scriptures in the course of a dozen chapters, its stress is thus on the *theology* of the composers and the nature of the *scriptural incarnation* in authors and texts of another time. Religion, history, politics or anything else is secondary to that purpose and the double focus.

A GUIDE FOR ADULT BEGINNERS

Every adult Christian at least has the right to such a meeting with the Word incarnate in the pages of the Old Testament (Jewish readers don't need reminding). A guide such as this should assist adult beginners to achieve it; those who have also an informed teacher to assist them, or are able to work in groups for mutual interchange, are at an advantage: the bread is best broken in community, and we are dealing here with the bread of life.

As we will make clear at every stage, a vast array of resources are available for further study when appropriate, especially as readers gain confidence; and it will be an intention of this guide to make readers increasingly independent by constant reference to such resources so as to enable them to go more deeply at will into the treasures of the Scriptures.

For a start, however, since the object is to meet the Word in the text, familiarity with the structure and text of the Old Testament is the opening challenge. For too many Christians, the Old Testament remains literally a closed book because they have never overcome the physical barrier of the text: mention of *Habakkuk* or *Nehemiah* sends them scurrying to table of contents or–admission of defeat!–page tabs, and this uncertainty can lead to avoidance. Unfamiliarity with the person of Jesus, Word incarnate, has likewise led people to ignore him. The loss in both cases is immeasurable, especially when we can quite simply guide people to the Word.

So now, like Augustine's response to the voice bidding him take up the sacred text and read (*Confessions* 8,12,29), let us begin reading it in some sort of illuminating order. Hopefully, the Word will be as liberating for us as for that other searcher after Truth.

Some relevant reading
R. E. Brown, *The Critical Meaning of the Bible*, London: Chapman, 1981
R. C. Hill, *Breaking the Bread of the Word. Principles of Teaching Scripture*, Rome: Pontifical Biblical Institute, 1991
Vatican II, *Nostra Aetate* (on Catholic attitudes to Judaism and the Old Testament)

CHAPTER 1

TEXTS IN
THEIR CONTEXT

AT YOUR OWN PACE

A meeting with the scriptural Word is what this guide exists to promote: it is not a substitute for it, nor can any other guide or introduction to the Old Testament be that. Hence our haste to introduce the reader to the text. For proper understanding of *Exodus* or *Proverbs* or *Judith*, however, to which we turn presently for reading, some account must be taken of the context in which the texts arose—just as understanding Jesus requires setting him in his times and culture. This is unavoidable, on incarnational grounds; but perhaps this chapter could be dipped into from time to time rather than read and conned as a whole, lest the reader faint in the way and not reach the precious text in which the Word speaks.

THE ANCIENT NEAR EAST

The world in which Jesus grew up, and earlier the authors of the Old Testament composed their work, mediating the Word to us, was different from ours. A truism? Yet modern readers of these texts do not always advert to that, or they are unaware of the differences and their reading of the texts is impeded. *Geographically* that part of the world has usually been called the ancient Near East—though that depends where you live. Some have to travel in a westerly direction to get to it, and it is certainly not near to everyone!

Our map shows the tiny country variously named Canaan, Palestine (after the Philistines), Israel (an ambiguous term) hugging the coast of the Mediterranean between generally larger countries like Egypt, Phoenicia, Syria, and across the desert Mesopotamia. The latter is a Greek term meaning "between the rivers"—Tigris and Euphrates. This is where Assyrian, Babylonian, Akkadian and Sumerian civilisations had developed. To people living today in the more isolated situations of Britain, the United States of America, Australia, this little country's placement seems uncomfortably fraught with the possibilities (still realized today) of conflict and interference, while on the positive side being open to *cultural and commercial*

3

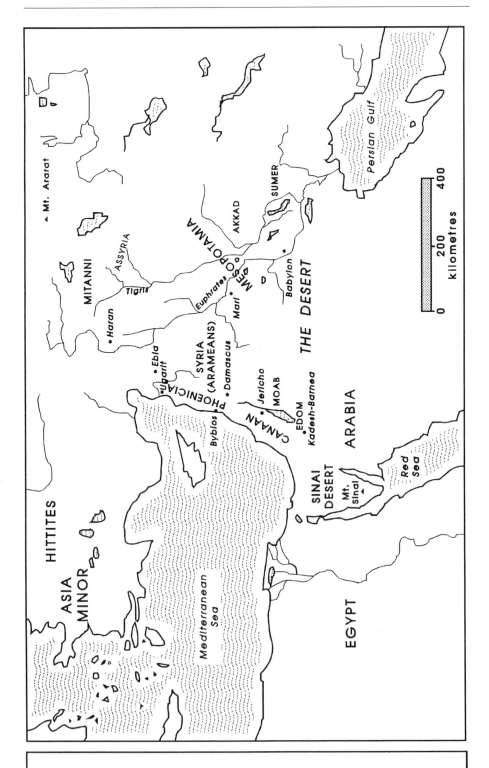

THE NEAR EAST IN THE BIBLICAL PERIOD

influence. Further to the West across the Mediterranean lay the peninsulas where Greek and Roman civilizations in their turn would rise. They would exercise decisive influence on the people who had finally settled in Canaan, prospered and eventually—under duress or by choice—sent out their members across the world, to add their bit to the literature and religion of the Jews, as they do today.

"A land flowing with milk and honey" it may have been to the biblical composers (cf. *Dt* 26.9), though to some of us it appears relatively dry and infertile. Still, the sweep of land that begins with Egypt, watered by the Nile, and moves north through coastal Canaan and Phoenicia and in crescent shape across through Mesopotamia down to the Persian Gulf, skirting the vast Arabian Desert at every stage, has been known as *the Fertile Crescent*. The patriarchs knew this in travelling by that route in search of food. We shall look more closely at climatic and other cultural features of the land of Israel in chapter 5.

The Fertile Crescent, in being a natural trade route, was also the path by which the people of Israel shared in a wider cultural interchange of the ancient Near East. Society, religion and—of particular significance for our reading—*literature* were affected by what the older, more powerful civilizations of Egypt and Mesopotamia and others had developed in their time. We can read today Hittite myths, epics from Ugarit, legal texts from Mesopotamia, Egyptian historical texts, letters from Mari and Elephantine, Wisdom material from many sources that have clear relevance to the work of our biblical composers, who in many cases betray the influence of this wider body of oriental composition. Our belief in the divine inspiration of our Scriptures does not preclude the role this whole cultural mix played in the formation of the Old Testament.

TEXT AND EVENT

The Old Testament, we have said, is not a history book—though obviously its composers come from different periods of Israel's history and reflect contemporary developments, even if writing about earlier events. We shall see many times that this is an important distinction to recognize in the case of Old Testament and any ancient authors—that is, the distinction between the *event* described and the author's *text* about it from a different period. Let us take some examples. The account of creation in chapter 1 of *Genesis* arises out of the exilic period around the fifth century and bears marks of that (see the timeline below). The relatively late report of Solomon's succession to the throne many centuries before that we find in *1 Chronicles* 28–29, composed for the benefit of a people returned from exile and in search of a model for a restored community, suppresses the

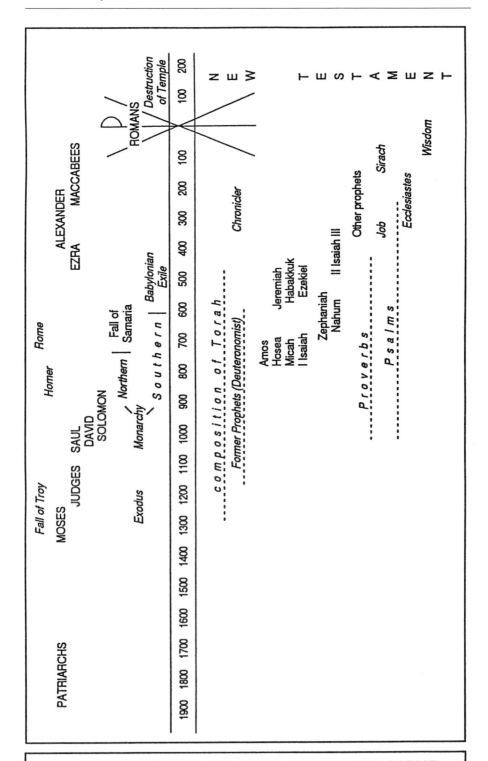

COMPOSITION OF THE OLD TESTAMENT
A timeline of key figures, events, authors

"warts and all" approach of the earlier version in *1 Kings* 1–2. The scepticism that affects Wisdom at a certain stage is related to the national rethink prompted by exile and return. And so on. So we need to be able to place composers and their texts in Israel's history as well as know the placement of events described.

The timeline offered here, "Composition of the Old Testament. A timeline of key figures, events, authors," should help bring out this important distinction and allow us to locate texts and events. (A formal history of Israel is not appropriate here; see references below to reputable history books.) The primeval history of the first eleven chapters of *Genesis*, of course, lies beyond any historical timeline. The patriarchal period dealt with in the remainder of *Genesis*, recounting the movements of the patriarchs through the Fertile Crescent and finally settling in Egypt under the Pharoahs, is only approximately dated and, of course, likewise has no eyewitness reporters in our Bible. With the rise of Moses, the Exodus of the Hebrew people from Egypt and their journey through the wilderness to a land of promise, we enter better documented history, probably the thirteenth century. Traditions about this foundational event would have been many and varied over the succeeding centuries. Only much later would they reach written form, in a technologically limited society, and take the shape we now know, perhaps as long as a millennium after the events. Further reason to keep in mind that distinction between text and event—a time-lag much greater than occurs in the compilation of the Gospels fifty years or so after Jesus, and yet the Gospels reveal considerable diversity of tradition.

Likewise, the literary work covering the story of the people from the conquest of Canaan in *Joshua* through establishment of the monarchy around a millennium before Jesus, division of the kingdom into Judah in the south and Israel in the north after Solomon, and the eventual fall of both states—the north to Assyria in 722 and Judah to Babylonia in 586—is completed in written form only then at the time of the Exile. We have to recognize how historical placement and theological purpose of such a later composer can affect the narrative we have in the books from *Joshua* to *Kings*. This emerges clearly by comparison with the approach to the same events by the even later composer of *Chronicles* working on this material in a different historical situation, namely, return from exile to a devastated Jerusalem. The text must be read in context: that is the constant message.

The prophets, too, are very much products of their historical situation, a fact that enables us to distinguish a variety of hands at work, for example, in the book of *Isaiah*. The eighth century prophet works in Jerusalem before the northern kingdom of Israel has met its fate under the Assyrians (chapters

1–39); the rest of the book is redolent of exile and return from exile centuries later, and comes perhaps from two other prophets. So prophets of eighth, seventh, sixth and later centuries reveal different concerns due in part to historical context. Northern origins cease to be a factor in our texts with the fall of Samaria in 722.

The arrival on the scene of the Greeks in the wake of Alexander's military successes brings to bear on Israel the religious and cultural pressure of Hellenization. This results in religiously motivated material like the *Maccabees* and *Judith* and a style of Wisdom that shows the influence of Greek philosophy, as in the *Wisdom of Solomon* in the last century before the New Testament. By the time of this latter work, the Romans have prevailed militarily in the region, though the culture remains Hellenistic into New Testament times.

OTHER RELIGIOUS LITERATURE

Within the country, as also beyond it in the Near East, religious composition of various kinds proliferated in the period after the Exile, as the author of *Ecclesiastes* laments in his dyspeptic way (12.12). Only a fraction of this Jewish composition made its way eventually into the rabbis' canon of the Hebrew Bible; Jesus and the New Testament authors know and quote from the wider range of 'intertestamental' literature (see ch. 14, "Literature beyond the canons"). Splinter groups like that on the Dead Sea at Qumran preserved the common texts, produced their own commentaries on them, wrote rules and propaganda of their own. In this early Judaism of the post-exilic period the rabbis themselves are developing a body of oral commentary on the Torah that will be codified as *mishnah* or "teaching" and will itself become the object of study, forming the *Talmud* and including also a style of biblical commentary, *midrash* (see Appendix 2, "Word and text"). Some little knowledge of this extrabiblical literature of the period will further help contextualize the texts we are reading.

So if we are to meet the Word incarnate in Old Testament texts, we must be aware to some degree of the *cultural conditioning* of these texts by the situation in which the authors lived and worked—their geographical situation, the cultural and particularly literary influences of the ancient Near East, the history of events and of reporters of events. As we began this chapter by observing, however, the primary challenge is not to bone up on a lot of geographical and historical information: the text must not disappear from sight, and much of the necessary information will emerge in our study of particular texts. We come to the Old Testament for *theological* reasons, not geographical, historical, cultural, etc. Otherwise, it would be like confining our study to the setting of Jesus' life and ministry,

and ignoring him. The principle of reading texts in their context has been
made sufficiently clear.

SOME BASIC UNDERSTANDINGS AND QUESTIONS

Further preparation for our task of meeting the Word incarnate in Old
Testament texts lies in some basic understandings we bring to this and
other literary material, and in some questions we can pose to whichever
text we are reading. The structure of the Bible is itself illuminating. It
would help, for instance, if we knew where the *Hebrew Bible* places those
two historical accounts in *Kings* and *Chronicles* we spoke of; both trace
events in Israel's history, but from rather different theological perspectives,
as we have explained above regarding Solomon's succession to David, and
placement in the Bible may reflect this.

Jewish people speak of their Bible's makeup under the mnemonic
TaNaK, short for *Torah-Nebi'im* (Prophets)-*Ketubim* (Writings). Torah, often
simply translated (by Christians) as "Law," refers firstly to the five books
that stand at the head of our Bibles, but gains a much fuller meaning for
orthodox Jews: "the whole body of belief, doctrine, practice, patterns of
piety and behavior, and moral and intellectual commitments that constitute
the Judaic version of reality" (Jacob Neusner, *Judaism in the Beginning of
Christianity*, Philadelphia: Fortress, 1984, 12). The Prophets include both
those figures the Christian Bible knows as prophets— "Latter Prophets,"
or "Writing Prophets," to the Jews—and also "Former Prophets," from
Joshua to *2 Kings*, who are prophetic because commenting on passing events
from a theological stance. It is interesting, therefore, that the reworking of
events in *Chronicles* to *Nehemiah* by the Chronicler is not included in the
Former Prophets by the Hebrew Bible, whereas the Christian Bible makes
no such distinction, classing both collections as Historical Books.

For the Christian Bible, only the Latter Prophets are called prophets,
and they are divided by length into Major and Minor; the minor, which
the Hebrew Bible calls the Twelve, number thirteen for us. This is because
we rather inappropriately include *Daniel*, which is really more apocalyptic
than prophetic. The Hebrew Bible places *Daniel* among the Writings, along
with other leftovers, like the Psalms, Wisdom books, *Ruth, Song of Songs,
Esther, Lamentations.*

THE STRUCTURE OF THE OLD TESTAMENT

HEBREW BIBLE	CHRISTIAN BIBLE
Torah	Pentateuch
–	
–	
–	
–	
–	
Prophets: Former	Historical Books
–	
–	
–	
–	
Prophets: Latter ('Writing')	Prophets
–	major
–	
–	
The Twelve	minor
Writings	Poetry and Wisdom
Psalms	
Wisdom	
Apocalyptic (Dn)	
Ruth, Esther, Lam, Ct	
The Chronicler	
	Deuterocanonical Books

The names of the Old Testament books differ from Bible to Bible, too. In our Christian Bible a Greek word normally summarizes the content of the book, like *Genesis, Exodus*—whereas the Hebrew Bible often prefers the opening or key words of the text: *Bereshith* ("In the beginning") and *Shemoth* ("Names"), in these two cases.

So the Christian Bible, which calls the Torah *Pentateuch* (Greek for "five scrolls"), arranges the books rather differently (as you will see from leafing through your Bible and from our table), on the model of the Greek Septuagint version. It uses a general category of Poetry and Wisdom to include compositions in verse, like the Psalms, which are only rarely Wisdom material. Also included in Bibles used by Catholics and Orthodox are those books removed by the rabbis from the wider collection of Writings known to Jesus—*1&2 Maccabees, Sirach (Ecclesiasticus), Wisdom (of Solomon), Judith, Tobit, Baruch*—and also classed by the Reformers as "apocrypha" (fictitious) and later removed. Catholics and Orthodox refer to them as "deuterocanonical" (canonical in a second category) books, and in these more irenic days everyone in fact reads them to gain an impression of the Judaism of those times (see ch. 3).

A further important understanding to bring to the study of the Old Testament, as of any literature of an earlier time and different culture, is a critical, evaluative, discriminating attitude so as to recognize the differences from our own time and habits. This is not "criticism" in the negative sense—just the evaluation true of all literary criticism, as we shall explain more fully in ch. 4. For instance, we have mentioned the need to concede the time gap between the events recorded from Old Testament history and their textual record. There is also an awareness of the particular type of "history" being composed in such records, which is more theological than historical in our modern, western sense (see ch. 6). We should also emphasize consistently that the biblical composers (in both testaments) are interested more in *truth* than in *facts*. The compiler of *Genesis* had no qualms about including two accounts of creation to give expression to different theologies—as the New Testament can accommodate two versions of Jesus' Great Sermon, Our Father, etc. A fundamentalist, failing to appreciate incarnation and its consequences both in the person of Jesus and the scriptural text, cannot allow for this critical attitude to the text, and remains uncritical, undiscriminating. To him or her any biblical text, like today's videotape, reproduces things exactly as they happened, in our terms and style.

There is a need, then, to examine the nature of biblical truth, and we shall do so in chapter 8.

Today we are being reminded that the texts of our Bible reflect a mentality that is largely male, that the composers we can identify are generally male. The texts chosen in chapter 8, for example, on "Divine Word, human word" show an insensitivity to the position of women in the ancient world. A reading of these texts should take these limitations into account. It would be an interesting exercise to turn our hand to rewriting such a text to eliminate this discrimination.

We should also be ready to acknowledge about our biblical texts that not only Jews and Christians have had their experience of God and written it up. We tend to read only our own scriptures, rightly holding for their "inspiration," God's role in their composition. Are we ready to concede that God has acted in the history of other communities and led them to record that in some fashion (though not in writing in many cases)? Perhaps, regrettably, we do not make ourselves aware of those other stories; but we can concede, while maintaining our Bible is the truth and nothing but the truth, that the *whole* truth about God's designs for all people (who are surely "chosen" too) and for the universe lies beyond the pages of one book and one history. A "biblicist" is one who sees biblical tradition—and one biblical tradition at that—as the only means of revelation being communicated to us.

The theme of this chapter, texts in their context, suggests we also address certain *key questions* to Old Testament texts we are reading. Where does the text occur in our Bible: is it part of Torah, a prophet from the Twelve, a piece of sapiential (Wisdom) material, one of the Chronicler's books? Is there general agreement on who the author was, or do we no longer know? Reference to one of the many good Old Testament Introductions should help us here. Does authorship determine the period in which the composer was working (as distinct from the date of the event recorded, of course)? Can we find some information about the sources used by the author/redactor for his purposes? Can we be sure where the author was working—for instance, are there signs of a prejudice against Jerusalem and the Davidic monarchy because of the author's northern origins? Is there evidence of later editorial work, perhaps by someone with similar prejudices?

AN EXAMPLE: READING *OBADIAH*

Let us take an example of how to read an Old Testament text, bringing these basic understandings and addressing these key questions to one book—in fact, the shortest book in the Old Testament, *Obadiah*.

Reading *Obadiah*

1. From our knowledge of the structure of the Old Testament, we turn to the Twelve to find the text of *Obadiah*. So we are reading one of the Latter Prophets, a fact which in itself is revealing: we will expect to find use of typically prophetic kinds of composition, such as the prophetic oracle, and prophetic themes, such as the Day of the Lord.

2. We read the brief text, which strikes us as rather spiteful, and seems to contain 1) an oracle from the Lord mediated by Obadiah against the nation of Edom, and 2) a prophecy of the coming Day of the Lord affecting all foreign nations.

3. The text tells us little of the author Obadiah, a suspiciously pious name *Obed-Yah(weh)*, "servant of the Lord." Because he is unsympathetic to Edom for its support of an assault on Judah

(by Nebuchadnezzar in 586?), we presume Obadiah is working in the wake of the Exile in Jerusalem for its community, who would relish this partisan material.

4. We check our map to see where Edom, a non-Israelite nation ("Esau" occurring frequently as a pejorative term), sits on the southern border of Israel. It is one of those nations known for its Wisdom tradition, to which Obadiah also scornfully refers. Reference to a History or an Introduction tells us Edom was finally conquered by the Nabateans in 312; so we can conclude Obadiah composed his brief work between 586 and 312.

5. We look for traces of later editorial work on the text. As the two parts of the work do not sit easily together, we may presume someone has combined them at some stage. Only an Introduction would alert us to the fact that vv. 5–6 resemble very closely *Jeremiah* 49.9–10, and vv 8–9, *Jer* 49.7; we can only conclude one author borrowed from the other or (more likely in this case) took from a common source.

6. We read the text again, savoring all we have learnt about author and contents, which helps bring together its rather scattered sections and explain its bitter tone. It is not one of the most winning parts of the Bible, we feel, resembling other prophetic material and some psalms (e.g. 137)—as also some New Testament "Woes". Yet it is a good sample of the complicated literary history of some Old Testament material, on which a good deal of work has to be done for a full understanding (like parts of Shakespeare, Homer, Virgil); flipping open the book may not always suffice.

A CHRISTIAN VIEWPOINT?

Do Christians read the Old Testament differently from Jews? Well, obviously, none of the Jewish Scriptures was composed with Christians in mind. Christians and Jews do share a conviction of the presence and activity of the Word of the Lord which, once spoken, "shall not return to me empty, but it shall accomplish that which I purpose" (*Isaiah* 55.11). What Christians feel able to do, in the light of the New Testament and with the explicit recommendation of Jesus, is to see a pattern developing in both testaments that St Paul will call the mystery of Christ. The Catholic community, less noted for its promotion of the Scriptures following the Reformers' accent on *scriptura sola*, has in recent times in a series of official recommendations come to encourage its members to get to know better the Scriptures Jesus knew, so that the Second Vatican Council in 1965 could say:

> *The Church has always venerated the divine Scriptures just as she has the very body of the Lord, since especially in the sacred liturgy she does not cease to take the bread of life from the table of both the Word of God and Body of Christ, and offer it to the faithful (Dei Verbum 21).*

At that Council a whole document was devoted to the Bible, including a chapter on the Old Testament. Contemporary Catholic theology and spirituality correspondingly reflect an acquaintance with this scriptural dimension of the mystery of Christ, even if the ministry of the Word in the community still requires much attention.

TEXTS, VERSIONS, MODERN TRANSLATIONS

We noted that the term "Hebrew Bible" is only partly an accurate description of the contents of the Scriptures Jesus knew, if simply from a linguistic point of view. There are parts of the Old Testament composed in the Aramaic language—whole chapters of *Ezra* and *Daniel*—which the people began using in place of Hebrew during the Exile in Babylon. These two semitic languages were related, somewhat in the manner that Italian is to Spanish. The wider canon now found in the Catholic and Orthodox canons also contains books composed in Greek (*Wisdom of Solomon, 2 Maccabees*), the language that Jews beyond and within Palestine used for official purposes during the Hellenistic period.

To such an extent, in fact, had Hebrew ceased to be a common language for the Jewish people after the Exile and such was the influence of Greek culture that long before the time of Jesus it had become necessary to provide Aramaic and Greek versions (or translations) of the Scriptures. The latter, called *Septuagint* ("seventy"; LXX in Roman numerals) because of the legend of the number of Greek translators, became widespread and served as the version the evangelists would have known when quoting the Old Testament. The Aramaic versions were called *targums*, as much paraphrase as close translation. Eventually, with the spread of the Roman empire and Christianity, Latin versions also developed, the official one being called *Vulgate* (in the sense of "commonly used")—though no Old Testament books were originally composed in Latin.

Scholars knowing the biblical languages and working on manuscript copies of original texts (no authors' copies, naturally, have survived to modern times) provide us with translations in our modern languages—the "vernacular", as we say. In English we have close translations, like the New Revised Standard Version and Jerusalem Bible, and freer translations, like the Good News. Our choice of a translation depends on the use we put it to—careful study as in our course at present or use with young people, for example. A critical bibliography will evaluate for us the wide range of available English translations (see also D. J. Harrington, *Interpreting the Old Testament*, 109–120).

AVAILABLE RESOURCES FOR OLD TESTAMENT STUDY

The Word, of course, spoken and in its textual form, is our principal resource; as the Lord says in Isaiah's oracle above, he is anxious that a meeting occur, and nothing should stand in the way of that. We on our side bring all of ourselves and our life experience to such a meeting; that too is a great resource for a fruitful encounter. Biblical study over the ages has produced a range of other aids to our efforts. A bibliography will list and evaluate them (such as Joseph A. Fitzmyer's *An Introductory Bibliography for the Study of Scripture*). Let us look at some of these aids:

We can leave to the scholars the use of a *lexicon* until we grasp a biblical language, though there are some popular works that try to help with the meaning of words. All of us can make use of a *concordance* (in English) that aims to list all the occurrences of a particular word, such as *holiness, covenant*, from which will emerge shades of meaning in different contexts. A *dictionary*, as distinct from a lexicon, will include entries on all matters referred to in the Old Testament, such as foods, customs, animals, seasons, etc.

What will be of most help in supplying answers to those key questions we raised above, such as authorship, sources, dating, literary structure, history of interpretation of particular books, is an *Introduction*. The name is deceptive: not an elementary text, it often gives very detailed information on these topics which can be a matter of debate among scholars, plus a bibliography. (The scriptural bibliography mentioned above will help evaluate the great number of Introductions that exist.) Once we have read the particular passage ourselves, it is time to enlist the help of experts; in our study of *Obadiah* above, only an Introduction enabled us to detect the verses *Obadiah* shares with *Jeremiah*, and it would supply as well the necessary geographical and historical background.

Taking up from where the Introduction leaves off in the task of getting us into the actual text is a *commentary*, going through the book chapter and verse at a time. There are many series of commentaries, pitched at various levels. The more sophisticated endeavor to help the *exegete* conduct *exegesis*: an explanation of the author's thought against the background of his time, touching on textual and linguistic matters, literary and historical issues. One is thus in a position to arrive at a statement of the author's vision and theological message. A commentary like *The New Jerome Biblical Commentary* not only comments on the text of each book in this way, but also supplies the background information usually offered by an Introduction.

We may have to look further for necessary detail—as in an *atlas*, for instance, or a *history* of biblical times, or an Old Testament *theology* that concentrates on the theological message of texts.

So there is an enormous amount of information about the Old Testament in print that we can turn to when appropriate, if we know where to find it (and that's part of preparation for the task). We should not think, however, that we are confined to the print media for resources. Other media of instruction have been developed in this "electric age," as McLuhan terms it, and biblical study has taken advantage of them: non-projected graphic media (such as charts and posters), projected visuals (filmstrips, slides, overhead projector transparencies), simple audio and audiovisual media (records, tapes, slide-tape presentations), films, TV programs, computers (including computer Bibles), databases (like CD-ROM, e.g. *Religion Indexes* One and Two).

A guide like this can simply point us in the direction of such riches—to be used only in service of our meeting the Word in the text, remember.

Scriptural bibliography

J. A. Fitzmyer, *An Introductory Bibliography for the Study of Scripture,* 3rd ed., Rome: Pontifical Biblical Institute, 1990; on a more modest scale S. B. Marrow, *Basic Tools of Biblical Exegesis*, 2nd edn, Rome: Pontifical Biblical Institute, 1978. For journal material see *Religion Index One* (now on CD-ROM).

Old Testament Introductions

Of the great range available, for our purposes the most suitable would be the *New Jerome Biblical Commentary (NJBC)*, ed. R. E. Brown et al., Englewood Cliffs: Prentice Hall, 1990, and the (abbreviated) *New Jerome Bible Handbook,* London: Chapman, 1992. For an Introduction that approaches the Old Testament not directly from the text but from biblical topics, D. J. Harrington, *Interpreting the Old Testament. A Practical Guide,* Wilmington: Glazier, 1981. (Fitzmyer's *Bibliography* evaluates the more sophisticated Introductions. In our text we refer you to those by Eissfeldt, Childs and others.)

Old Testament commentary series
Beyond the *NJBC*, there are the *Old Testament Message* (Wilmington: Glazier), *Daily Study Bible* (Edinburgh: St Andrew's Press), *Cambridge Bible Commentary* (Cambridge: CUP) series; the *Old Testament Library* (London: SCM) and *Anchor Bible* (Garden City: Doubleday) are more advanced (see also Fitzmyer).

Old Testament history
B. W. Anderson, *The Living World of the Old Testament*, 3rd edn, London: Longman, 1978 (in U.S. *Understanding the Old Testament*) gives a good historical (and geographical, cultural, . . .) setting to Old Testament texts. J. Bright, *A History of Israel*, 3rd edn, Philadelphia: Westminster, 1981, is standard (see Fitzmyer's comments).

Atlas of Old Testament times
J. A. Rhymer, *Atlas of the Biblical World*, Melbourne: Macmillan, 1982; R. E. Brown, *Recent Discoveries and the Biblical World*, Wilmington: Glazier, 1983.

Other literatures
J. B. Pritchard (ed.), *Ancient Near Eastern Texts Relating to the Old Testament*, 3rd edn, Princeton: Princeton University Press, 1969, gives texts from earlier cultures (generally known as *ANET*; a mini-*ANET* [1958] is also available). For intertestamental literature, H.F.D. Sparks (ed.), *The Apocryphal Old Testament*, Oxford: Clarendon, 1984; for Qumran texts, G. Vermes, 3rd edn, *The Dead Sea Scrolls in English*, Harmondsworth: Penguin, 1988; for rabbinic commentary, A. Cohen, *Everyman's Talmud*, New York: Shocken Books, 1975.

Old Testament theology
Anderson, *The Living World of the Old Testament*, highlights the theology of the authors he examines; Fitzmyer evaluates some of the more formal Old Testament theologies, like those of G. Von Rad, W. Eichrodt, and W. Zimmerli, *Old Testament Theology in Outline*, Edinburgh: Clark, 1978. (Best to avoid those, like Rowley, Jacob, and Vriezen, which impose the categories of Christian theology on Old Testament material.)

Scholarly surveys
Periodically, volumes appear presenting the current state of Old Testament scholarship, mainly on the literature but also on history, archeology, etc. *The Hebrew Bible and its Modern Interpreters*, ed. D. A. Knight and G. M. Tucker, Chico CA: Scholars Press, 1985, is one such. An earlier but still

valuable one is G. W. Anderson (ed.), *Tradition and Interpretation*, Oxford: Clarendon Press, 1979.

Journals
These have the merit of keeping us up to date periodically with developments in biblical study, and vary in their degree of specialization; for our purposes the simpler *The Bible Today, Biblical Theology Bulletin, Scripture Bulletin* will help.

Audiovisual material
Unlike print media, there is no definitive catalogue; producers of AV material on the Bible are listed in Hill, *Breaking the Bread of the Word*, 142–144.

ABBREVIATIONS

For convenience, names of the Old Testament (like New Testament) books are abbreviated in references in some such way as this:

Gn	Genesis	Sir	Sirach (Ecclesiasticus)
Ex	Exodus	Is	Isaiah
Lv	Leviticus	Dt-Is	Deutero (Second)-Isaiah
Nm	Numbers	Tr-Is	Trito (Third)-Isaiah
Dt	Deuteronomy	Jer	Jeremiah
Jos	Joshua	Lam	Lamentations
Jgs	Judges	Bar	Baruch
1–2 Sam	1–2 Samuel	Ez	Ezekiel
1–2 Kgs	1–2 Kings	Dn	Daniel
1–2 Chr	1–2 Chronicles	Hos	Hosea
Ezra	Ezra	Joel	Joel
Neh	Nehemiah	Amos	Amos
Tob	Tobit	Obad	Obadiah
Esth	Esther	Jonah	Jonah
Jdt	Judith	Mic	Micah
1–2 Macc	1–2 Maccabees	Nah	Nahum
Job	Job	Hab	Habakkuk
Ps(s)	Psalm(s)	Zeph	Zephaniah
Prv	Proverbs	Hag	Haggai
Eccl	Ecclesiastes (Qoheleth)	Zech	Zechariah
Ct	Canticle of Canticles (Song)	Dt-Zech	Deutero-Zechariah
Wis	Wisdom (of Solomon)	Mal	Malachi

You will find abbreviations in scholarly books for other texts of the period, versions, modern translations, journals and the like. A key to most is found at the beginning of the *New Jerome Biblical Commentary* [*NJBC*]). Some common ones are:

LXX	Septuagint ("Seventy" [translators], for the Greek version of the Old Testament)
ET	English translation
JB	*Jerusalem Bible*
KJV	*King James Version*
(N)RSV	(New) Revised Standard Version
ms(s)	manuscript(s)
Grk	Greek
IDB(Supp)	*Interpreter's Dictionary of the Bible (Supplement)*
ANET	*Ancient Near Eastern Texts*, ed. J. B. Pritchard (see above)
AB	*Anchor Bible* (series of commentaries)
Dtr	Deuteronomist
OTL	*Old Testament Library* (series of commentaries)
OTM	*Old Testament Message* (series of commentaries)
JSOT	*Journal for the Study of the Old Testament*
CBQ	*Catholic Biblical Quarterly*
PACE	*Professional Approaches for Christian Educators*
TBT	*The Bible Today*
BTB	*Biblical Theology Bulletin*
Int	*Interpretation*

A REMINDER

Remember, all this information is meant to facilitate a response to the principal challenge: your meeting the Word in the text. It should not impede it. So we suggested at the opening of this chapter: dip into this *at your own pace*, according to need. Don't let mere fact–finding hold up the process of reading the Word. To that we now turn.

CHAPTER 2

▼

SERVANTS OF THE WORD

**texts: *Exodus* 19–24 and *Deuteronomy* 5–8; *Proverbs* 15–20
biblical topic: authorship and composition
theological theme: choice, promise, election**

We begin getting acquainted with the biblical Word by taking lengthy passages from major sections of Hebrew (and Christian) Bibles: Torah (Pentateuch) and Writings (Wisdom). Both these works would have had a prominent place in Jesus' upbringing, for they are classic statements of the Jewish way of life and its basis in law and in experience.

We choose them also because we want to see biblical authors at work in communicating the Word. It is good to avoid referring to them as "writers," considering the limited technology available and the processes involved in transmission; "authors," ("composers") is non-committal about the way the traditions were passed on.

In reading these texts and others in each of the next twelve chapters, remember to follow the process we outlined above in regard to *Obadiah*:
1) read the text slowly yourself, trying to let as much as possible sink in;
2) then turn to a good Introduction you have access to so as to acquire necessary information scholars over the years have gained about the text;
3) finally reread the text in the light of the further information.
This should ensure a fruitful meeting with the Word incarnate in the text.

Exodus 19–24 and *Deuteronomy* 5–8: the giving of the Law

1) Check the place of these books in the Bible, and recall the definition of "Torah" by Jewish scholar Jacob Neusner back on page 9: all that is meant by the Jewish way of life.

   Read both passages in your Bible, preferably of the close translation type (like *NRSV* or *JB*) that will reveal more accurately resemblances and differences between texts and, in this case, the characteristically exhortatory, repetitive style of *Deuteronomy*. You would note that both passages describe the same event and material, though in somewhat different ways; so you presume different reshaping of a similar tradition by different composers. This impression is confirmed by slight cases of repetition and contradiction within one narrative and between the narratives. For example, there are different names for the mountain, a different order of the Ten Commandments. It is clearly the solemn moment of the giving of the Law to the people in the person of Moses, and (in the case of *Exodus*) the ceremony of covenant ratification with "the blood of the covenant"; echoes of this narrative we remember in our Christian liturgy. The people of Israel are in the wilderness on the way from Egypt to the land of promise, and have arrived at the mount of Sinai (or Horeb in *Dt*).

2) Turn to an Introduction (such as the *NJBC*, its *Handbook* or some other Old Testament Introduction you have available) for further light on the texts and the (much earlier) events they describe. Reference to our timeline above and maps will help pinpoint events and later text, and also the great length of time taken to put the Torah in final form. There will be mention of various hypotheses by scholars to explain the double narratives and their unusual features; various hands are clearly at work here, and some Introductions will even attribute individual verses to contributors variously named *Yahwist, Elohist, Priestly* composers, and in the case of *Deuteronomy* a different author (see Appendix 3, "Pentateuchal criticism"). In what sense Moses is author of all this material we shall discuss in our "biblical topic" below.

   From a *theological* point of view we also note the centrality of the Decalogue/Ten Commandments in both passages in the Book of the Covenant, which these passages have been called, and the wider context in which the Commandments sit. Whereas Christians have been accustomed to extract ten commands in abbreviated form and neglect the whole message, we note (with assistance from commentators) that the Lord's statement comes in a fivefold *covenant form:*

1. Historical prologue: "I am the Lord your God who brought you out of the land of Egypt, out of the house of slavery";
2. General commands (our "Ten Commandments");
3. Particular commands—about shrines, slaves, kinds of crimes, etc;
4. Blessings for observance; and
5. Cursings for inobservance.

That certainly puts a different complexion on what might otherwise appear to be arbitrary regulations from a dictatorial overlord. Instead, we are invited to respond to a Lord who has already acted mightily in our behalf. We thus see the whole package as significant, especially when commentators suggest that the oriental treaty/covenant under this form is but a figurative way of expressing a relationship Yahweh wants to have with his people—and should be taught that way, not simply as ten Do's and Don'ts.

3) We read the texts again, noting the different styles of different contributors, appreciating the positive character of the Book of the Covenant as a whole, with its accent on love and genuine concern (especially in *Deuteronomy*). We situate the Decalogue within the total document, realizing now that "testament" is but a legal figure for an intimate relationship between one God and one people.

In chapter 6 we shall examine the central place of covenant in Old Testament—as in New Testament—theology.

Further reading
Appendix 3, "Pentateuchal criticism"
B. W. Anderson, *The Living World of the Old Testament*, 81–97
J. J. Roberts, "Law, covenant," *The Hebrew Bible and its Modern Interpreters*, 92–94

Proverbs 15–20

1) In reading these proverbs, we realize we are clearly in a different world from the Torah. Firstly, they stand within the Writings/Poetry and Wisdom sections in our Bible. Again, while they are as concerned about morality as the Book of the Covenant, the material is far from being covenantal morality—no mention of divine voices, Moses, mountain, wilderness, tablets. One point of resemblance is that here too there seems a variety of hands at work, a collection of aphorisms all in

proverbial form but some less terse than others, some repeating or even contradicting others. Remove half a dozen, and they would not be missed. This feature is accentuated when we note that *Proverbs* consists of a number of such collections, our chapters occurring within "The proverbs of Solomon" beginning at chapter 10.

The atmosphere is much less rarefied than before. We are dealing with the stuff of ordinary life—children and parents, speech and gossip, passing bribes and falsifying weights. It is not the God of the patriarchs and Sinai who is warning us of these things but human experience; "the fear of the Lord" is popped in occasionally as a rather pat sentiment. There are also occasional references to kings and courtly behavior. The proverb (Hebrew *mashal*) is the typical form of Wisdom expression. Some of these quaint, unconnected proverbs have survived into modern times (e.g. 16.18), when we have developed a great number of our own (think of some). There is plenty of mention of "wisdom" and "the fountain of wisdom," but the range of interests here is much wider than the quality of being wise: we are dealing with Wisdom material, sapiential composition (Latin *sapientia*, wisdom), which we shall see has a whole range of characteristics that constitute a Wisdom perspective or worldview, distinct from (e.g.) Torah or prophecy (cf. Appendix 4, "Biblical Wisdom").

2) When we turn to our Introduction, we find that the book of *Proverbs* as a whole consists of half a dozen or so collections of proverbs from different periods and different backgrounds. We are informed that other cultures had their Wisdom material, which has been thought to have left its mark on this book and even on our chapters (see also ch. 1 above, "The Ancient Near East"). The date of the material in these chapters within "The proverbs of Solomon" and its relation to King Solomon (whose reputation for wisdom was international: look up *1 Kings* 4.29–34) is uncertain, but it could be as old as the monarchy. The complete book was put together centuries later, in post-exilic times. Authorship of *Proverbs* is clearly complicated.

3) Read the chapters again, a proverb at a time, not looking for sequence or consistency. Appreciate the different origins of this material from Torah material, its different religious character, the popular roots of the sages. Can you understand why for a period the Wisdom books were neglected by Old Testament scholars, and why they have come back into favor? What would be lost if the Bible did not have such sapiential composition? Can you see how Jesus absorbed much of the content and style of his Wisdom scriptures?

Further reading
C. R. Fontaine, *"Proverbs," The Women's Bible Commentary* (ed. C. Newsom, S. Ringe), London: SPCK, 1992, 145–52
R. E. Murphy, "Introduction to Wisdom literature," *NJBC* 447–452
R. C. Hill, "The perspective of Wisdom," *Scripture Bulletin* 21 (1991 July) 16–20

BIBLICAL TOPIC: AUTHORSHIP, COMPOSITION

Reading these chapters from Torah and Writings of the Hebrew Bible, and learning some details of the books' background, have alerted us to a fact that is basic to an understanding of the Old Testament. It is something that Jesus in his time and culture would have taken for granted but that we have to acknowledge as not being true of literary composition today. Composition of ancient texts is more complex for various reasons; it is a complexity that the uniformity of printing conceals in our Bibles, where every passage of every book looks like any other.

Variety of hands

We have highlighted in Torah and *Proverbs* the variety of hands at work in composition of a text now presented to us as a literary unity. When we glance at our timeline (p. 6) we appreciate that in the long history of compilation before each work reached final form there was a greater degree of community involvement than is true of most of our published works today. Some of the biblical proverbs are age-old; but then many of ours are, too. Even in biblical history, law, prophecy, poetry in the form that has come down to us, contributors are more numerous during the process of composition than readily appears. It is rarely possible to nominate one single author of a biblical work—and that would be true of New Testament "books," too. Jesus and his contemporaries would accept that more easily than we would.

Oral transmission

This complexity, variety, richness of background to an Old Testament work or passage arises also from the fact that many of those contributors are involved in oral transmission of traditions, legends, beliefs, laws. We have to keep reminding ourselves of the more limited skills, materials and technology available to Old Testament composers: leather, metal, linen are not user-friendly materials, let alone tablets of stone! Writing is not common until a millennium before Jesus, and difficult even then; the biblical prophets deliver their oracles by word of mouth, and rarely mention writing them down (cf. *Is* 8.1; *Jer* 36). The process from oral composition, literary incorporation and eventual editing into a final form could take many hundreds of years, as in the case of the Torah, the Former Prophets, *Proverbs, Psalms*.

Development of tradition

The length of this process gives rise to something we note also in the Gospels despite their relatively rapid movement (50–60 years) from story to text—namely, diversity of tradition. The greater the time span, the higher the chance of development/alteration of transmission, or tradition, of the material. We can hardly expect traditions about such remarkable events as the Exodus and the plagues (which *Deuteronomy* keeps classing as "signs and wonders, great and grievous") not to undergo elaboration in the process of (oral) transmission over the ages. Many a good story is improved in the telling, and our beliefs about biblical inspiration and biblical truth do not commit us to think such elaboration occurs only outside the Bible.

Degrees of responsibility

Today authorship generally means composition by one person, though "ghost writing" and other forms of shared responsibility (not always acknowledged) also occur. In more "primitive" societies where writing was a less simple matter, where composers did not always see their composition through to a final form, we have to allow for various degrees of responsibility for composition. Even in the New Testament what we know as Paul's letters were the result variously of dictation, ghost writing, tacit approval instead of the busy apostle's total responsibility for every written word. So it is more likely that in the Old Testament a nominated author cannot be held responsible for every word we now have; chapter 36 of *Jeremiah* shows the prophet's secretary taking down dictated material but with such freedom that "many similar words were added to them" (v. 32).

Pseudonymous authorship

Nor are we to think that an author's name placed at the head of a work in its final form is an exclusive attribution. *Proverbs* is attributed to Solomon, that exemplary figure of wisdom, and this is appropriate; yet the text also acknowledges other contributors (cf. chs 30, 31), and we can be sure all those age-old aphorisms, like our own today, derive from a variety of sources. The ancient practice of pseudonymous authorship lent respectability to a literary composition; so to figures of eminence in a particular field works would be attributed, like David for his psalmody and Moses as the pre-eminent lawgiver. Hence only in a certain respect do we accept the Mosaic authorship of the Torah in the face of clear evidence of diversity of contributions. Jesus would use "Moses" in this sense or even as author of all the Old Testament (cf. *John* 5); it is a theological, not a literary judgment.

A fundamentalist approach to the biblical Word is impatient of recognition of these incarnational factors of composition of biblical texts; far easier simply to listen to the Word speaking and take the texts at face value. Unfortunately, the reality is that God's Word comes to us in human words—just as in Jesus the Word comes to us in the human condition. Not to recognize the features of literary composition by servants of the Word (in both testaments) is equivalent to ignoring that other incarnation of the Word in Jesus.

Further reading
Vatican II, *Dei Verbum*, ch. 3
D. J. Harrington, *Interpreting the Old Testament*

THEOLOGICAL THEME: CHOICE, PROMISE, ELECTION

Before you begin your study of this particular theological theme, you should read what is said in Appendix 5, "Old Testament theology," which treats the whole topic. There we are reminded once again that what is given us in the Bible is *theology*, not history, religion, sociology or anything else found in other ancient literature. Theology has been defined as "faith seeking understanding"; and in the Old Testament we are reading the efforts of people like Job and The Chronicler to make sense of what their *faith* tells them of God acting in their situation. We try to recognize their insights into God's plan; in this way the Word speaks to us. Sometimes we can see the whole divine plan; sometimes we have to settle for individual theological concerns of the authors.

We begin with one such theological theme here—a basic one to every Jewish community: being chosen by God.

We suggest you read the Old Testament passages below to illustrate the various features of each topic. Read aloud, if possible, because rhythms are often significant and characteristic.

A PEOPLE CHOSEN

The people who gave us the Old Testament have no doubt that they are no ordinary people but one specially chosen, elected, to whom particular promises are made. Though the Greek title *Deuteronomy* means literally a second (version) of the Law, the text shows that it is more a personal relationship with God than mere legal requirement that is involved—relationship arising out of God's choice and covenant love (*Dt* 7.6–11). The *Psalms* celebrate this fact: God chose Israel/Jacob/us (e.g. *Ps* 47).

BY THE LORD AS THE LORD'S OWN

One of the classic statements of the choice of this people by Yahweh (the name their God reveals to them: cf. *Ex* 3.14) is the message given to Moses for transmission to them on Mt Sinai in the desert (*Ex* 19.1–6): Yahweh has borne them up on eagles' wings, and if they keep their part of the covenant relationship, they will be his special possession. The prophets will remind the people that this choice entails response on their part, as *Hosea* does through his characteristic marriage imagery (2.16–23).

ON THE BASIS OF RACE

These promises as mediated to later ages in the people's literature make no secret of the fact—or at least the composers' interpretation—that on one racial group, children of Jacob (or Israel, the nickname given him in *Gn* 32.28) the choice falls; we saw Obadiah belittling the Edomites as sons of Esau, not Israelites at all. This racial exclusiveness did not lessen in the minds of some composers even at a late stage: the sage Ben Sira sees the great gift of wisdom conferred especially on Israel (*Sir* 24.1–12).

ABOVE ALL OTHERS/TO THE EXCLUSION OF OTHERS?

The position and future of other racial groups in Old Testament theology is generally negative: "You only have I known of all the families of the earth," Yahweh says to Israel in *Amos* (3.2). Oracles against "the nations" are common in early prophetic literature, and would have been welcomed by a people under pressure. After the Exile, however, some composers take a wider view of the scope of divine salvation (*Jonah* is the conspicuous example), even if Israel has a key role in their redemption (*Is* 42.1–9).

CHOSEN IN THE PATRIARCHS, TO WHOM THE PROMISE WAS MADE

Abraham and the other patriarchs are the founding fathers of this privileged community; to them the promises were made (as *Genesis* 12 begins to tell). In them the people became objects of choice; to them as to the people it was said, "Do not be afraid, I am with you" (*Is* 41.8–10).

FOR SPECIAL CARE, PROTECTION, LOVE

Choice entailed love and care: the Old Testament, though often misrepresented as conveying forbidding images of God portrays God as the 'tender parent dealing lovingly with Israel as an often disobedient child (see *Hosea* ch. 11). "You are precious in my sight, and honored, and I love you," the Lord says to Israel (*Is* 43.1–7).

AND THUS ENJOYING MANY MATERIAL BENEFITS

The Old Testament people felt that divine choice was the cause of their arrival in a land of milk and honey; it was a promised land. Even before their loss of the land and many material benefits, they had to be reminded that these benefits were not of their making—"a land with fine, large cities that you did not build"—as *Deuteronomy* (7.12–16) and *Joshua* (24.13) point out to them. Material prosperity becomes a sign of divine blessing.

AND RESPONDING TO THIS ELECTION BY FIDELITY

Covenant of the Sinai type was bilateral: protection by one party entailed fidelity by the other—this is basic to the Old Testament prophetic message in particular. The lengthy *Psalm* 119 on covenant and law reinforces the need for such fidelity by the people (vv 57–64). The fact that the continuance of the material benefits of election also depended on the people's fidelity to Yahweh is also stressed (*Dt* 6.1–3).

OR RISKING THE LOSS OF PROMISE BY INFIDELITY

The worst possible scenario for the Jewish people, therefore, is the cancellation of the covenant: "Do not break your covenant with us," pleads Jeremiah, who admits the overwhelming infidelity now leading to Exile (14.11–22). It is in fact the Exile that gives the people the opportunity to reflect on this possibility; the long homily/prayer in *Nehemiah* 9 surveys all salvation history on this theme of divine fidelity/Israel's infidelity from the viewpoint of the returned community.

Further reading

S. Terrien, *The Elusive Presence. Towards a New Biblical Theology*, San Francisco: Harper & Row, 1978, 63–105

C. Westermann, *The Promises to the Fathers* (1976), ET Philadelphia: Fortress, 1980

EXERCISES

1. Are you accustomed to speak of biblical "writers"? Do you see how this can be a misleading practice? Why, specifically, could it lead to a misunderstanding of the material you have read in *Proverbs* in particular?

2. In reading the passages from *Exodus* and *Deuteronomy*, what differences did you detect between them? Make a list of these. Can you see how different hands have worked similar material differently? Does the *Further reading* touch on this?

3. List half a dozen proverbs you are familiar with in daily use. How do these compare with the biblical proverbs, and in what ways do they differ from the legislative material you have just read from the Torah?

4. Can you see how the Old Testament people, in thinking and speaking about their election as a specially chosen people, have theologised about their faith and arrived at a pattern of divine behavior (favorable to them)?

CHAPTER 3

▼

THE COMMUNITY'S RELIGIOUS TRADITIONS

texts: *Judith 10–14; 1 Maccabees* 1–4
biblical topic: canon
theological theme: slavery, deliverance, EXODUS, freedom

Within his own religious community Jesus listened to and read the traditions of that community handed down in the texts we know as the Old Testament. As we noted, those texts had undergone modification in the course of transmission, and their collection was also a matter of development. Students of the Judaism of Jesus' time remind us that it was then not one homogeneous group with one already determined collection of scriptures. Later, sixty years after Jesus' time and in the wake of the cataclysmic event of the sack of Jerusalem and destruction of the restored Second Temple, leaders of the once more embattled community would further modify its scriptural tradition on grounds thought relevant in the circumstances. The followers of "The Way" (as Jesus' disciples within Judaism came to be known before Luke's time: cf. *Acts* 9.2) would continue to take advantage of the wider heritage.

Scholars helping us interpret the Jewish Scriptures suggest that, while appreciating the varied activity of the servants of the Word we have just looked at under the aspect of authorship, we need to consider also and primarily the fact of community acceptance. Whatever is true of the background and processes of their composition, we should read the texts as the religious literature of a community and appreciate each within that religious literary whole. So, in reading the Torah, we concern ourselves less with its complex composition than with its vital role in the life of the religious community. Orthodox Judaism today would provide a lesson in that type of reading.

One reservation about this canonical approach is that it is hard to be definite about *the* community receiving the sacred text. The restored community in Jerusalem for whom the Chronicler composed, the community under siege from the Greeks, Jesus' community taxed by Caesar, the community for whom the rabbis of the 90s provided—all received the

Word differently. What was critical for those resisting Hellenistic persecution (we look at two examples in *Judith* and *Maccabees*) could seem irrelevant and even fanciful at a later time. Every judgment or yardstick (*kanon* in Greek) is to some extent affected by the contemporary situation. We have preferred to stay with the Scriptures Jesus knew as being acceptable to his community.

Judith 10–14 (remember to follow the three stages of reading)

1) There is no doubt this is colorful material, the stuff "biblical" movies are made of. There is that unbeatable mix of religion, sex and violence—not unique in the Bible, of course, or beyond it. We find it hard to take seriously the extremes of the piety of Judith ("Jewess"), obviously a religious model, and her prowess with a sword, albeit in the best of causes. She can lecture the villainous general Holofernes on God's purposes for her people (11.10) and plot his downfall in precise detail.

   We are further alerted to the composer's moral and symbolic purposes when we note his clearly deliberate falsification of historical detail: though the story purports to tell of the invasion of Judah under the Babylonian Nebuchadnezzar, the enemy are called Assyrians, the great power dislodged previously by the Babylonians. And if we turn to the beginning of the book, we find a hopeless mish-mash of Assyrian, Babylonian, Median and Persian names and places that any contemporary reader would know was concocted to discourage them from treating this as straight history.

2) Yet even we clearly perceive the religious and moral message the writer is conveying under this pseudohistorical guise, and this leads us to surmise its purpose and perhaps circumstances of composition. The model Jewess, with her devotion to the God of Israel, Mosaic Law and Temple cult in the face of foreign aggression and pagan pressure, is obviously meant to be an example to a people under similar pressure from some foreign culture later than the Persians—perhaps the Greeks. Nothing is known about the author beyond these doctrinal positions within the text, suggesting pharisaic authorship in Hellenistic times, in Hebrew, perhaps early first century.

3) We read the chapters again, accepting the strong message of fidelity the author is giving to a community under pressure to defect, recognizing the curiously independent part played by this ideal woman who can uphold Law and at the same time practice deception, behead despots, put the males of the community to shame. Not too many women in

Israel are accorded the accolade, "You are the glory of Jerusalem, the great boast of Israel, the great pride of our nation" (15.9)! Could that be a further reason for the book's later exclusion from the Jewish canon? Its religious value for its own community (and ours?) is not in doubt.

Further reading
J. Craghan, *Judith et al.* (OTM 16)
O. Eissfeldt, *The Old Testament. An Introduction*, 585–87

1 Maccabees 1–4

1) Two things strike us on reading these chapters: the more avowedly historical approach in conveying a similar religious message to *Judith*'s, and some mystification as to why later rabbis might consider such well constructed (albeit nationalistic) history to be unacceptable to their community. The complications of canon and community are becoming more obvious.

   The opening of our text helps us relate its content and composition to our timeline (p. 6). Jewish resistance to the inroads of Hellenistic culture and military might under Alexander the Great's successors is accounted for; we are left in no doubt as to whose side the author is on. The villain of the piece is Antiochus IV, offensive enough even without his assumed title "God in person," *Epiphanes*; the hero is Mattathias, of the priestly Hasmonean family and founder of a dynasty that would be called also Maccabean from his son Judas's nickname. We are formally introduced to all the main characters in these chapters, the battle is joined, and good triumphs over evil as in all good religious history. Like *Judith*, the religious message of fidelity to Torah and tradition is patent.

2) This time, however, the facts have not been fudged. This time we get *facts* and *truth*. Though the author does not have a name, his sympathies with Judaism and the Hasmoneans are overt. The original was in Hebrew, it seems. We have only the Greek version, which is probably what the rabbis also had, to their further dissatisfaction. The author is writing within half a century or so of the events described—although we can be sure of direct recording in textual form only, not oral. In later chapters he quotes sources, chapter and verse, that he found in the Temple archives. (What is now *2 Maccabees* is an earlier composition.) Despite his obvious bias, as history his work is unexcelled in the Bible and in the Hellenistic period generally.

3) A second reading concentrates on the religious message in prose and verse. We regret that the book's very precision historically could be a

reason for the later Jewish community's finding it unacceptable for being too late. They thus forfeited material which would clearly have been very edifying for the community of the composer and has much to offer their successors and us today.

Further reading
N. J. McEleney, *"1–2 Maccabees"*, *NJBC* 421–446
J. Collins, *Daniel, 1–2 Maccabees* (OTM 15)

BIBLICAL TOPIC: CANON

It has become clear already that the yardstick or *canon* applied to a community's normative traditions, including written traditions, is rather a sliding scale that responds to the developing situation of the community. What is fixed at one time may become more or less flexible under different conditions. (For Catholics, Canon Law shows the same development.) Various religious communities—Jewish, Catholic, Orthodox, Protestant— have their own canons of Scripture, and of Old Testament in particular, which have changed over the ages. "Scripture is defined as authoritative writings, whereas the canon is restricted to a dogmatic decision through which the limits of Scripture are defined and fixed" (B. S. Childs).

Various norms

The various norms that influence the formation of scriptural canons include *chronology, language, doctrine, geography, politics, authorship*. A community may decide a certain date is critical for completion of authentic material; for instance, a view within Judaism in the early Christian period that the prophetic spirit ceased with Ezra (in about the fifth century before Jesus) led to exclusion of some later books—and inclusion of others thought erroneously to be earlier (like *Jonah, Daniel, Ecclesiastes*, parts of *Isaiah, Zechariah, Esther*)! Composition in Hebrew or within Palestine could also be critical at a period. A doctrinal tangle over a book's contents (like the doctrine of purgatory for Luther) could also become a sticking point. Naturally, these norms are susceptible of development over time.

Qumran scriptures

Judaism, as we have seen, did not settle on its scriptural canon until after the time of Jesus. A century or two before him the community at Qumran on the Dead Sea were reading books that were later not included in the

Writings (like *Sirach* and *Tobit*), whereas the collections of Torah and Prophets evidently had been finalized. On the other hand, *Esther* is not found at Qumran, probably for theological and liturgical reasons.

Narrower canon

Jesus too knew the wider canon. And the New Testament composers include references to the deuterocanonical books, as well as to three or four others. It took a couple of centuries of the Christian era for the Jewish community to settle on the narrower canon we now know as the Hebrew Bible, under several influences. There was the idea put forward in contemporary influential writings that Ezra's role was decisive. That had the effect of excluding some books like *Sirach*, which admits its second century date, and including others—sometimes in error! *Daniel*, for example, is also probably second century but purports to be much earlier, which was a common procedure.

After the sack of Jerusalem and destruction of Herod's restored Temple in 70, a pharisaic group of rabbis moved west to Jamnia on the coast, from where they are credited with a role in forming the canon over the years. In this period doubts were held about the place in the canon of *Ezekiel*, *Song of Songs, Ecclesiastes* and *Esther* for doctrinal reasons.

Christian canon

The Christian community had similar hesitations, both within and beyond Palestine—though it is not accurate to speak, as some do, of a "Palestinian canon" on the model of the later Hebrew Bible, and a wider "Alexandrian canon" preferring the contents of the Septuagint. St Jerome is said to have favored the rabbis' selection, St Augustine the latter—though our criterion must instead be what was known to Jesus. By about the fifth century there was general consensus about the wider canon in both East and West. Eastern Orthodox communities today generally accept it.

Protestant canon

The canon generally adopted in Protestantism goes back to 1519, when Luther in debate with Johann Maier of Eck on the question of purgatory rejected the testimony of *2 Maccabees* by appealing to Jerome's ranking of some books as *deuterocanonical* as distinct from those accepted even by the rabbis, *protocanonical*. These books (*1&2 Maccabees, Tobit, Judith, Sirach* [*Ecclesiasticus*], *Wisdom of Solomon, Baruch* and parts of *Esther* and *Daniel*) Luther now called "apocryphal," though retaining them as "useful and good for reading"; later reformist groups would exclude them from the Bible altogether. The Council of Trent (1545–63) on the basis of consistent Church usage reaffirmed the canonical status of both protocanonical and deuterocanonical books defined by earlier councils, but excluded as *apocryphal* others known in Protestant Bibles today as *pseudepigraphical* (e.g. intertestamental books).

There is therefore quite a discrepancy in the terminology employed: we said canon is a messy business. Yet in today's less polemical atmosphere people read all such scripture as the religious literature of a community, or several communities. Protestant scholars are in the forefront of this rethink. We are thus healthily less exclusive in determining where the Word is speaking to us.

Further reading

A. C. Sundberg, "Reexamining the formation of the Old Testament canon," *Interpretation* 42 (1988) 78–82

J. A. Sanders, *Canon and Community*, Phildadelphia: Fortress, 1984
———————— "Canonicity," *NJBC* 1035–43

THEOLOGICAL THEME: SLAVERY, DELIVERANCE, EXODUS, FREEDOM

(Be sure to read—aloud, if possible—the passages nominated below.)

THE PEOPLE WERE OPPRESSED AND ENSLAVED IN EGYPT

Exodus 1.8–14 is the classic statement of the fact of enslavement. An ancient "cultic credo" occurs at *Deuteronomy* 26.5–9, so called because reciting beliefs in a (para)liturgical situation, like our creeds; it too highlights the hardships of oppression in *Deuteronomy*'s characteristically repetitive style.

THEY WERE DELIVERED BY THE LORD

Psalm 135 insists that deliverance came from the Lord alone. The prophet Ezekiel, both upbraiding and encouraging the exiles in Babylon, gives the same assurance (20.1–10). His version of the period of slavery has the epiphany of Yahweh, which other accounts normally assign to the wilderness experience, occurring in Egypt. He also characteristically attributes the deliverance to God's desire to vindicate the holiness of his name.

THE MARVELS OF THE EXODUS

Nothing so riveted itself on the community's imagination as the marvels that accompanied the Exodus. *Exodus* recounts them in detail in prose, then includes another version (15.1–18) variously entitled the Song of Moses, Song of Miriam (cf. 15.21), Song of the Sea, which being in verse is probably of ancient origin. Much later The Chronicler rehearses them (*Neh* 9.9–11) in his lengthy survey of salvation history. They are fresh in the mind of other biblical authors as well (as they are in the Christian liturgy).

THE PLAGUES AFFLICTING THE EGYPTIANS

One striking detail of "the signs and wonders, great and grievous" of this divine action was the number of plagues that beset the Egyptians. *Exodus* 12.29–32 recounts briefly but pathetically the death of the firstborn, from the child of Pharaoh who sat on his throne to the firstborn of the prisoner who was in the dungeon. For an elaboration of this, in the manner of *midrash* we find the author of the *Wisdom of Solomon* 18.5–13 with the same text in front of him, teasing out its emotive potential.

THE RITUAL OF PASSOVER: CELEBRATING MOVEMENT FROM SLAVERY TO FREEDOM

The ritual was already in practice for centuries by the time of composition of our classic text, *Exodus* 12.21–27, which reports Moses' directions about the ritual and looks "ahead" to the time of later celebration to guarantee proper understanding. *Deuteronomy*, later again, is likewise conscious of the need to understand a by now hoary practice: the further "cultic credo" (6.20–24) appropriate in such liturgical situations acknowledges that children in particular may not realize fully the significance of details of the Passover celebration.

THE EXILE: ANOTHER ENSLAVEMENT

The biblical authors make much of the fact that the insufferable fate of slavery befell the people again in the Babylonian Exile. To be captives again in a foreign land is more than the psalmist can bear: *Psalm* 137 shows all the desperation and pathos of a tormented exile. The morally inclined "historians", of course, appreciate the irony of the reversal of fortunes in the Exile, like The Chronicler's long sermon/prayer (*Neh* 9.32–37)—even on return the community laments, "We are slaves to this day."

RETURN FROM EXILE: ANOTHER EXODUS

Prophetic voices in the Exile can see a positive side to it: deliverance as of yore. Second Isaiah, whom Zimmerli called "that impressive evangelist," proclaims the good news: "a path in the mighty waters" is possible again (43.14–21). The author of *Baruch*, purporting to write to the exiles (probably from a much later period of oppression), beautifully describes the way this new Exodus will occur (5.1–9).

ENSLAVEMENT TO SIN ALSO INHIBITS FREEDOM

To the morally inclined a further experience of slavery always lay within reach: enslavement to sin. The *Psalms* frequently evoke the language and situation of Egyptian captivity to warn of the dangers of relapse (*Ps 81*), the need of divine help to avoid this (*Ps 38*), and the plight of those who thus forfeit their freedom (*Ps 7.14–16*).

DELIVERANCE FROM SIN IS ALWAYS AVAILABLE

On the Lord's side there is continuing readiness to bring out of slavery those who fall back into sin, if they repent: that is a staple prophetic message. *Hosea* 2.14–17 evokes the Exodus language to promise restored relationship "as at the time when she came out of the land of Egypt." Jesus in the Nazareth synagogue will restate this generous offer by quoting the words of Third Isaiah (61.1–4) proclaiming "the year of the Lord's favor."

For the Jewish people, only the Holocaust (*Shoah*) of modern times could parallel the Exodus as an event of such far-reaching national significance. It too has been the subject of theological evaluation by the community, similar to that which we detect in Old Testament texts on the Exodus.

Further reading

B. W. Anderson, *The Living World of the Old Testament*, 41–74

P. Doron, "The motif of the Exodus in the Old Testament," *Scripture Bulletin* 13 (1982 No. 1) 5–8

EXERCISES

1   Which Bible translation are you working with? Does it have all "the Scriptures Jesus knew"? Check the Table of Contents for all the books it contains.

2. How did you respond to the chapters from *Judith*? What indications did you detect of the author's religious purpose? Can you think of non-biblical material that uses historical incidents for such a purpose?

3. Does a similar bias appear in *Maccabees*? Compare it with *Judith* for a closer adherence to historical fact.

4. In what way does Christian worship reflect the importance the Old Testament gives to the Exodus in that people's history and belief?

CHAPTER 4

AN ABUNDANCE OF
CONTRIBUTORS

texts: *Song of Songs; Isaiah 52–53*
biblical topic: biblical criticism
theological theme: desert, wilderness

In our approach to the Old Testament we use the term "Mosaic authorship" to refer to the role the great prophet played in literary composition, of the Torah in particular. We saw it is a complex question. We could also speak of "mosaic authorship" of many other texts in the sense of the variety of materials employed in assembling a complete work, like ancient and modern mosaics in the graphic arts. Because of the antiquity of these Old Testament compositions and the tradition, often oral, of earlier elements, it is rarely we can speak of a single contributor involved in producing the work we now read. Not only were original authors part of this process, but so too were the more ancient sources on which they drew—and these latter were also perhaps derivative. We noted the similarity of some of the *Proverbs* to earlier Egyptian parallels, as a glance at *ANET* on Egyptian Wisdom texts will further demonstrate (Pritchard gives marginal cross-references to Old Testament texts). Finally, the work of the original author(s), in oral or written form, became community property and subject to alteration by later contributors over a long period, not always preserving consistency.

Old Testament works, of course, are not unique in this regard; the Gospels, too, reveal multiplicity of contributors, as does other literature. To read Shakespeare's *Henry VIII* is to come up against the puzzling shift in loyalties the text betrays at a certain stage: the writer seems to move from support of Catherine against Henry to rejection of Catherine and support of Henry and Anne. Reference to a Shakespearian "Introduction" unearths the fact that the original text was damaged by fire in the Globe theatre and rewritten by another playwright, evidently with different sympathies.

We are grateful to the critics who help us recognize the variety of contributors to the work we are reading, from those who unearth damaged texts (like Shakespeare's) to those who apply literary skills to detection of various authors'/editors' contributions. Each has affected the message we receive from the Word.

Song of Songs

1) This remarkable biblical work has all sorts of effects on readers who come to it after a diet of historical or prophetical material. Some are scandalized, or pretend to be. (An elderly fellow Catholic, who would not have been raised on the Bible, once challenged me: "You wouldn't let children read that dirty book?") Other readers, including many young adults I teach, find its inclusion within the covers of the Bible quite enlightening and liberating. Even the great German commentator Eissfeldt remarks, "Here we have profane love songs and wedding songs, as they are to be found in all the world and always will be."

All of us can share the mixed feelings of the early Jewish and Christian communities about the appropriateness of this material and how to take it. The New Testament never quotes it, and Rabbi Akiba cursed those who still sang verses from it in wineshops!

The Old Testament gives this book Solomon's authority: "the song of songs (canticle of canticles, in Latin) of Solomon," or Solomon's best song of all. We know from looking at *1 Kings* 4 that Solomon had a reputation for songs ("one thousand and five"!) and proverbs, so that attribution made it more respectable than the local bards. When we read it, we thrill to the presence of such unashamedly human, sexual emotions and descriptions in the various poems. Does that say something of our expectations of the limits of religious expression? It is very redolent of the culture of an ancient oriental agricultural, even nomadic people, whose images are of vineyards and flocks and herds, for whom nard and myrrh were vital for a pleasant fragrance (in place of washing?). We wonder how to take it: at face value as boy-meets-girl love songs, or a figurative way of treating divine love, that relationship between God and his people for which the Torah uses instead a political figure?

2) It is no surprise that the question of interpretation has remained open from the beginning. Some parts may be as old as Solomon, others have late Aramaic and other terms and usage. Were they all secular love songs taken over for religious purposes, or always religious in function—perhaps at an allegorical level, whereby each person and thing has a spiritual meaning? Or is it perhaps a drama in which Solomon woos the girl, or tries to take the girl from her lover? Jews and Christians are at one in giving this very poetic material a religious value, the former employing it in worship at Passover. Are we Christians more hesitant to do so?

3) Reading it again allows the lushness of the imagery to wash over us and perhaps permits us to see how deserving it is of a place in our Scriptures, those that Jesus knew. Whatever its origins, we can appreciate its religious character in the whole canon of the Old Testament, helping to balance more arid material. The total effect could not have been anticipated by its many contributors; hence the rabbi's irritation with those who took it back to the winebars.

Further reading

O. Eissfeldt, *The Old Testament. An Introduction*, Eng. trans., Oxford: Blackwell, 1965, 483–91

R. E. Murphy, "History of exegesis as a hermeneutical tool," *BTB* 16 (1986 No 3) 87–91

M. Pope, *Song of Songs (AB* 7c)

Isaiah 52–53

1) We find *Isaiah*, of course, at the head of the Latter Prophets. Glancing at our timeline we notice mention is made of more than one Isaiah; the first is at work in the eighth century, the second (Deutero-Isaiah) and third in the wake of the fall of Judah in the sixth. The opening verses of these chapters suggest an exilic setting, the prophet comforting the exiles with the good news of a return to Jerusalem in the manner of the Exodus of old, the Lord going before them and in their rear. Then there is a sudden switch to a long poem, in a quite different mood, about "my servant" who will suffer for many transgressors though himself innocent. We recognize echoes of the poem in our liturgy (not to mention Handel) and its similarity to the situation of Jesus in the New Testament.

2) Scholarship clarifies the date and setting of this prophet working in Babylon and his relationship to Isaiah of Jerusalem (responsible for chs 1–39) and to Third Isaiah (56–66) writing to returned exiles. We are also told of the occurrence in the text of Second Isaiah of four songs or poems about a mysterious servant of Yahweh, including this one, 52.13–53.12. The identity of the servant seems to vary between the nation Israel, the prophet, even the Persian king Cyrus who allowed the exiles to go free. In our song the servant is perhaps the prophet who is to suffer for the people. Before the time of Jesus Jews interpreted the song, when at all, messianically, i.e., with a view to future realization of community hopes (see ch. 13, "Looking for someone to come"). But their messianic hopes had no place for expiatory suffering; the song was largely ignored by the community at Qumran and also by official

Judaism, and the targums (Aramaic translations) downplayed the sufferings of the messiah, whereas the New Testament has Jesus applying it to himself. An editor who sensed the relationship of prophets centuries apart finally combined their work (existing in oral and written form) in the book we now have—surely an abundance of contributors.

3) Reading the chapters again we can see the prophet's overall purpose in his situation, but (like many other scholars) still puzzle over the connection between the song and the whole thread of his work. We appreciate why the New Testament would find the figure of "the lamb led to the slaughter," bearing the sin of "many" (who are they? Jews only?), so suited to their understanding of Jesus. We try to keep this Christian interpretation to one side; our concern here is to study the theologizing of Old Testament authors—as Jesus did.

Further reading

J. J. Roberts, "Isaiah in Old Testament theology," *Int* 36 (1982), 130–43

C. Stuhlmueller, "Deutero-Isaiah," *NJBC*, 329–42

J. Jeremias, *The Eucharistic Words of Jesus*, ET London: SCM, 1966, 227–231

BIBLICAL TOPIC: BIBLICAL CRITICISM

The readings from poets and prophet have reinforced our awareness of the richness coming from the many layers and voices that make up biblical text. The Word that comes to us from the text is surely polyphonic, and our hearing must become attuned to that multiplicity if we are not to miss the richness. Critical reading will help us be attuned. We are using "criticism" in that positive sense of evaluation, judgment, discernment. Our example from Shakespeare shows that all literature, especially from a past age, can benefit from such discernment.

Accepting the Incarnation

As we stated in chapter 2 on the process of biblical composition, our *theological* justification for applying these principles of general literary criticism to the Bible is basically the Incarnation: the Word comes to us in all the richness and limitations of the human condition. To fail to grapple with the human aspects of the text, as fundamentalists are loath to do, is to downplay the humanity of the Word incarnate—in Jesus and in the text. For the Catholic community the Second Vatican Council, accepting from early Church Fathers the insight into this double incarnation, recommended close attention to *human* factors of composition (like the abundance of contributors) if the *divine* message is to be recognized fully.

> *Since God speaks in sacred Scripture through human beings in human fashion, the interpreter of sacred Scripture, in order to see clearly what God wanted to communicate to us, should carefully investigate what meaning the sacred writers really intended, and what God wanted to manifest by means of their words* (Dei Verbum *12).*

Skills and techniques

There are various critical skills and techniques available to students of the Bible (as of any other literature). They have generally been referred to as tools of "historical criticism" because they take account of development in the transmission of the material (asking, for instance, about the origin of the songs of the Suffering Servant now found in the text of *Dt-Is*). At times they have been classified under areas of "lower criticism" or "higher criticism".

TYPES OF BIBLICAL CRITICISM

"Lower criticism"
- archeology (discovering the materials)
- textual criticism (evaluating the manuscripts, once found)
- language skills (reading manuscripts, once evaluated)

"Higher criticism"
- literary criticism
- source criticism (the author's sources)
- redaction criticism (the use of sources)
- structural criticism (discerning patterns in the material)
- form criticism (use of pre-formed genres, forms)

Biblical scholars are continually profiting from advances in other kinds of literary studies to apply further forms of criticism to the text of the Old Testament. We shall advert to these in chapter 14, "Further critical approaches."

Keeping a balance

To profit from the work of historical critics and others, as our reading of *Song of Songs* and *Second Isaiah* was enriched, we must heed the reminder given at the end of chapter 2: do not let critical detail make us lose sight of the text. We must meet the Word primarily, not his commentators. There is a balance to be kept if we are not to go to one extreme as fundamentalists have gone to the other.

Further reading
John J. Collins, "Methods and presuppositions of biblical scholarship," *Chicago Studies* 17 (1978 No 1) 5–28

Fortress Press, Philadelphia, has published series of *Guides to Biblical Scholarship* for both Old and New Testaments, the former series edited by G. M. Tucker including titles such as *Form Criticism of the Old Testament* (G. M. Tucker), *Historical-Critical Method* (E. Krentz), *Literary Criticism of the Old Testament* (N. C. Habel), etc. Some of the New Testament series are also relevant (e.g., *What is Redaction Criticism?* by N. Perrin).

THEOLOGICAL THEME: DESERT, WILDERNESS

(Be sure to read—aloud, if possible—the Old Testament passages nominated below.)

THE PEOPLE'S WILDERNESS EXPERIENCE FOLLOWED THEIR DELIVERANCE

The book of *Numbers* describes the people's experiences in the desert following their Exodus from Egypt. It lasted forty years, says the text in mentioning Aaron's death on the verge of their entry into Canaan (33.38-39). The Priestly account of the wilderness period (see Appendix 3, "Pentateuchal criticism") composed in Exile centuries later is stronger on theology than on fact, so we should look rather for theological significance in details of the narrative, like the number of years.

IT WAS A TIME OF PERFECT UNION BETWEEN THE LORD AND THE CHOSEN PEOPLE

A similar idealized theological interpretation of the experience can be found also in the prophets, for their own purposes. Hosea, calling the people of the north to fidelity on the model of a perfect marriage, speaks of the Lord's loving converse with the people in the wilderness and their ready response at that time (*Hos* 2.14–15). Jeremiah, perhaps influenced by Hosea, transmits an oracle of the Lord likewise to Judah recalling their devotion in the wilderness in terms of covenant love (*Jer* 2.2–3).

IT WAS A PERIOD OF CONVERSION

Both these prophets see the time in the desert also as a conversion experience that serves as a contemporary paradigm. Hosea urges the north to turn from affluence to pristine desert conditions that favored intimacy with the Lord (12.8–9). Jeremiah, with return from Exile in mind, speaks of the people's "finding grace in the wilderness" as in the past because "I have loved you with an everlasting love . . . I have continued my faithfulness to you" (31.2–3).

IN THE DESERT THE PEOPLE EXPERIENCED GOD'S POWER AND LEADERSHIP

The tradition about that period contains memorable experiences of divine power, which that homily (of Ezra?) in *Nehemiah* recounts: the pillar of cloud and the pillar of fire, the epiphany and Sinai covenant, bread from heaven and water from the rock (9.12–15). They are likewise an obvious motif of hymns of praise and petition (e.g. *Ps* 68).

AND ALSO YAHWEH'S CARE FOR THEM

For his prophetic purposes Hosea reminds the unfaithful north of God's constant offers of loving care after "calling my son out of Egypt," which they spurned, even though he "bent down to them and fed them" (11.1–5). The Song of Moses now sitting in the text of *Deuteronomy* 32.10–14 speaks at length of God's care for the people in "a howling wilderness desert waste" where God nursed, fed, guided them like an eagle hovering over its young—all to no purpose.

WHICH WILL BE REPEATED FOR THE EXILES IN BABYLON

Second Isaiah begins his Book of Consolation with a comforting promise to the exiles that what happened before in the Exodus and in the desert will happen also to them (*Dt-Is* 40.1–5). It is another theologically idealized picture of the way of the Lord running straight through the desert, and the revelation of the glory of the Lord, which the New Testament will see realized not only in the exiles' return but especially in the coming of Jesus.

IT WAS ALSO A PERIOD OF TRIAL WHICH THE PEOPLE FAILED

Less romantically, and probably more in keeping with the facts as *Exodus* and *Numbers* recount them, the desert experience proved to be a time of challenge to fidelity which the people did not measure up to. Hosea can admit as much along with his idealizing, contrasting powerfully God's choice of the people ("like grapes in the wilderness")—there and not in Egypt, as usually—and their adoption of Canaanite fertility gods.

MANY MISUNDERSTOOD AND REGRETTED THIS OPPORTUNITY

To the people the opportunity to undergo an experience of divine care in the wilderness was not an unmixed blessing; in fact, many would have passed up the opportunity so as even to return to slavery in Egypt. *Exodus* (17) and *Numbers* (20) both report the incident at Massah, or Meribah, where thirst leads to complaints about the point of it all; the *Psalms* likewise make much of this lack of appreciation (81; 95).

Further reading
B. W. Anderson, *The Living World of the Old Testament*, 75–81
S. Talmon, "Wilderness," *IDB Supp*, 946–49
D. Bergant, "The Desert in biblical tradition," *TBT* 31 (1993 No 3), 134–40

EXERCISES

1. Are you familiar with the neutral use of the word "criticism", as in biblical criticism, literary criticism? Or do you bring a negative sense to a "critical" approach to Old Testament texts? Are you content to be thought a critical reader?

2 What was your first reaction to reading *Song of Songs*—surprise, shock, enjoyment, relief? What does this say of your expectations of the contents of a Bible? Are they realistic expectations?

3. How did you respond, as a Christian, to the Servant Song in this passage from Second Isaiah? Can you appreciate how the New Testament authors have called upon it? Read the other songs at 42.1–7; 49.1–7; 50.4–9; are they alike?

4. Have you had the opportunity of a wilderness experience? Why was it important for the Old Testament people, and why is such an experience valuable for us all?

CHAPTER 5

LIFE AND CUSTOMS

texts: *Ruth; Joel*
biblical topic: culture of ancient Israel
theological theme: the Land

As in our approach to Jesus, we need in reading the text of the Old Testament to acknowledge that biblical characters and composers lived in a fashion different from our own. Their life and their customs which emerge in the ancient texts that we read are not identical to ours. A visit today to the lands of the Bible will help bring this home to us, but only partially. We will note the features of the small country of Israel, the climate, seasons, agriculture.

It is an effect of incarnation—true also in the person of Jesus—that such conditions may not be ours, and that we have to make an adjustment in our thinking if we are to recognize the message in its fulness. A people of that time and character will think and pray in images and symbols we may not be familiar with. The worldview of that people we have long gone beyond. Social and political arrangements will also differ from ours today. Let us read a couple of Old Testament texts in which these cultural features are prominent.

Ruth

1) The placement of this charming, quaint story about filial piety raises an initial question for us. In our Bible *Ruth* sits among the Historical Books, and in fact seems rather out of character with that material, despite the opening and closing historical sketches. The Hebrew Bible (cf. outline on p. 10), on the other hand, does not admit it among the Former Prophets but relegates it to the Writings, evidently not seeing it as historical in that sense. Perhaps the rabbis were also not anxious to promote a foreign woman, albeit one who finds Yahweh (a glance at our map shows Moab on Israel's eastern border). We on the contrary warm to the unusual openness to other peoples (and willingness to place

women at center stage: Ruth and particularly Naomi come across as resourceful characters). Agricultural practices, Boaz's reaction to Ruth's advances, the right of redemption are interesting cultural features of the time.

2) Scholarly opinion is uncertain about the date. The Septuagint in tacking the book on to *Judges* and before *Kings* was obviously influenced by the opening reference to the former times and to David's lineage respectively, though perhaps that closing genealogy is an addition. The universalist attitude to foreigners is usually thought late (like *Jonah*, as we saw), and perhaps the involvement of a foreigner in David's line was meant to offset the concern about intermarriage after the community's return from Exile as seen in The Chronicler. As often, the work is anonymous.

3) We read it again as a pious story making a few moral and theological points. We can appreciate how different biblical compilers—the LXX and the rabbis—could place it differently in the Good Book. Its cultural features lend it a further quaintness. We note that today's hymn writer has not quite respected the sense of Ruth's words, "Wherever you go . . . " We also wonder: who is the principal character, Ruth or Naomi?

Further reading

S. Niditch, "Ruth," *The Hebrew Bible and its Modern Interpreters*, 451–456

A. Levine, "Ruth," *The Women's Bible Commentary*, 78–84

P. Trible, *God and the Rhetoric of Sexuality*, Philadelphia: Fortress, 1978, 166–99

Joel

1) This book occurs among the Twelve, or in Augustine's phrase, the "minor prophets". We are familiar with parts of it from the Lenten readings urging us to repent. What prompted the call to repentance was not so clear to us from those readings: it was in fact a plague of locusts, which readers from the country will confirm is very accurately described, suggesting the author knew it well. But he also is familiar with details of Temple worship, so perhaps exercised his prophetic ministry there. Who he was is sketchily stated; his name *Jo(Yah)-el*, "Yahweh is God," is suspiciously pious but does occur elsewhere.

We have some difficulty seeing the final chapter or so about the judgment of the nations on the Day of the Lord cohering with the earlier part of the short book, though it too has some agricultural references. We begin to wonder if the author has a real locust plague in mind.

2) Comparing *Joel* in our Bible with some other versions reveals differences in numbering chapters and verses. The Hebrew had four chapters, Greek and Latin combined chapters 2 and 3 to leave us with three chapters (which our *NRSV* has, like most English translations [Luther further complicated things by combining instead chapters 3 and 4]). The author may be a cultic prophet. Dating is difficult: the Temple is standing, but no reference is made to the court; so perhaps it is post-exilic after the rebuilding of the Temple in 515 but before the destruction of Tyre and Sidon (still standing in the text) in the late fourth century. Some suggest the two parts of the book, dividing at 2.28 (*NRSV*), are from different authors.

3) We read the whole book again, allowing for the possibility that the author (for all his close knowledge of the land) is employing the wonderful description of the locust plague along with the later vision of Israel sitting in judgment on the nations as one piece of apocalyptic (see chapter 11 for more on apocalyptic): the nation will arise from catastrophe to a noble destiny. We can relate the movement from black despair to glorious prediction to a type of homiletics we have all experienced in certain preachers today (or yesterday). It is moving, the more so that its religious message arises partly from the prophet's own knowledge of agriculture and liturgy.

Further reading

K. S. Nash, "The cycle of seasons in *Joel*," TBT 27 (1989 No 2) 74–80
J. Kodell, *Joel et al.* (OTM 14)
G. M. Tucker, "Prophecy and the prophetic literature," *The Hebrew Bible and its Modern Interpreters*, 325–68

BIBLICAL TOPIC: CULTURE OF ANCIENT ISRAEL

It has been remarked that the biblical characters (and composers) played their part on a small stage. The narrow strip of land, once called Canaan, that they occupied on the Mediterranean coast (see map, "The Near East in the biblical period," p. 4) covered about 7000 sq. miles, thus being about the size of Tasmania or the state of Massachusetts. Even today it does not strike the visitor as a particularly fertile country, though being part of the loop of land called the Fertile Crescent that skirts the desert from the Nile in Egypt through Israel and around into Mesopotamia,

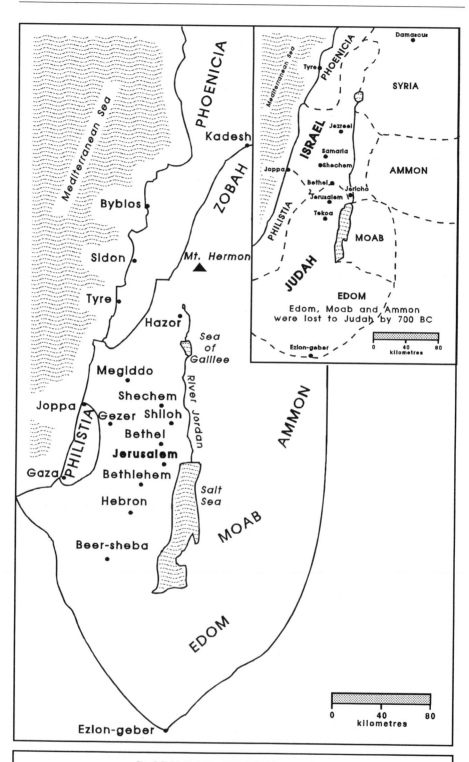

DAVID'S KINGDOM
(inset) Israel and Judah divided

watered by the Tigris and Euphrates. The land is irrigated only by the river Jordan flowing from the Sea of Galilee south about 70 miles to the salty Dead Sea (below sea level).

Israel's fertility is affected by climatic conditions. Rainfall is relatively sparse, varying from 25 inches near the coast to a mere 5 inches on the east bank of the Jordan bordering the desert, and less around Jericho and the Dead Sea. No rain falls during summer, when the temperature reaches the 40s (Celsius) around the Dead Sea, especially when hot desert winds blow; it is cooler in Jerusalem in the hill country of Judea, and snow falls on Mount Hermon on the northern border.

Seasons

The seasons in this country are, of course, those of the northern hemisphere. January and February are the coldest months. The rain comes with spring (*Joel* welcomes it: 2.23; cf. *Hos* 6.3), and the desert blooms—a complete, longed-for transformation. Crops ripen rapidly by early summer; then drought and heat set in, and the vegetation withers. Autumn brings some rain to break the drought for sowing.

Calendars

For this agricultural people the year began with the rains of autumn permitting the sowing of crops; the Jewish civil New Year is still observed in autumn, even though later ecclesiastical calendars followed a Babylonian system of twelve months beginning in spring and based on the cycle of the moon, therefore requiring an additional "intercalary" month every five years. The day began at sunset (that is why Jesus' Last Supper and Crucifixion occurred on the same day). The great sacred festivals, originally agricultural but later linked to historical events, were: Passover (combining lambing and barley harvest festivals, later linked to the Exodus); Weeks/Pentecost (end of the wheat harvest, fifty [Greek *pentecostos*] days after Passover, later linked to the Sinai covenant), Booths/Tabernacles (end of the agricultural year, linked to the wanderings in the wilderness). Other festivals came to include the Day of Atonement, Dedication and Purim. The Sabbath was itself an occasion for strict observance.

To the nomadic Hebrew people who entered Canaan from the wilderness the land seemed prosperous, a land of milk and honey (cf. *Dt* 26.9). To a farmer, however, agriculture would be a backbreaking challenge, the land barren and rocky, especially away from the plains. Only on gentler slopes and plains could grain crops be grown (and then at risk from plagues such as Joel recounts); vines, figs and olives could cope with rougher conditions. The growing season is short and growth brisk. Water is scarce, and had to be stored in underground cisterns, unless a spring provided "living water." Sheep and goats roamed the hills, raised for meat and milk, wool or rough hair for clothing, leather for wineskins and other domestic uses.

Living conditions

Living conditions were not easy for this nomadic people turned farmers. Most were engaged in agriculture during Old Testament times, as is clear from their festivals, their laws, and the images occurring in the Old Testament. Failure of crops could lead to the farmer having to sell himself and his family into servitude. For self-defense and access to water supplies people also lived in towns; under David Jerusalem developed into a large city, and worship was centralized with the construction of the Temple under Solomon. Houses were largely of stone in a country where little timber grew.

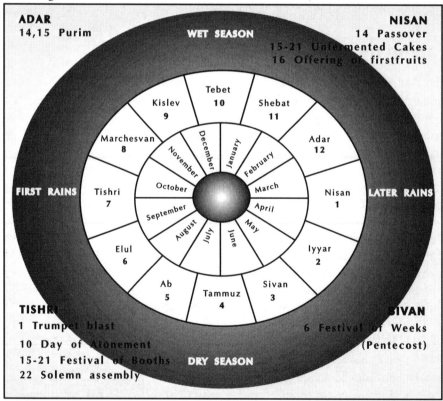

Jewish calendar and seasons

Social organization

Only with David did the Old Testament people achieve nationhood, and soon afterwards the people of Israel divided into two kingdoms, Israel in the north (thus leading to ambiguity in usage) and Judah in the south. Before David there were families, clans and tribes. But even from the time of the Exodus they could be described as one religious community, God's own people, united in worship—a theocracy, with a common belief system centered on the Exodus and Sinai experiences. Families were linked from early times in the clan, an extended family involving rights of property such as *Ruth* describes. The twelve tribes (listed differently in different Old Testament books), if not in fact originating from the twelve patriarchs, were later assigned to them.

Images and symbols

The images and symbols of Old Testament literature are those of an agricultural people once nomadic: light and darkness, bread and wine, blood and water, day and night. For the Hebrew people God is life-giving water; he is a fortress and a rock.

View of the cosmos

The Old Testament reveals a view of the cosmos different from what we have been able to arrive at. For the Hebrew people God created the earth resting on its foundations amidst a shapeless expanse of waters. It was protected from these waters above and below by a "firmament"; in this firmament or dome were windows that allowed some water to fall as rain. Beneath the earth at the foot of the mountains there was a great pit or cavern known as *sheol*, into which the dead go and from which there is no return.

Further reading
T. A. Pearson, "Biblical foods and eating customs," *TBT* 27 (1989 No. 6), 372–78

P. Perkins, "Women in the bible and its world," *Int* 42 (1988 No. 1), 33–44

D. Baly, *Basic Biblical Geography*, Philadelphia: Fortress, 1987

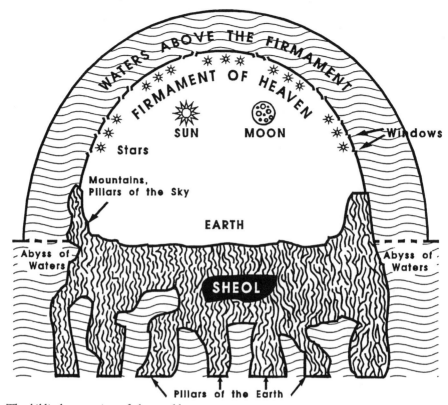

The biblical conception of the world

THEOLOGICAL THEME: THE LAND

(Be sure to read—aloud if possible—the passages nominated below.)

A PROMISE MADE TO THE PATRIARCHS

In the earliest traditional statements in the Old Testament a promise of land was made to the patriarchal figures. The ancient "cultic credo" that is now in our text of *Deuteronomy* 26.5–9, like that at 6.20–24, speaks of the land in those terms, and is introduced by the worshipper's words to the priest, "Today I declare to the Lord your God that I have come into the land that the Lord swore to our ancestors to give us." The giving of that promise in the case of Abraham is recounted in the text that opens the Yahwist's patriarchal history, *Genesis* 12.1–3, where the patriarch is bidden to "go to a land that I will show you."

THE GOAL OF THE PEOPLE'S WANDERING IN THE DESERT

The Torah continues to present the Lord insisting to the people in the wilderness that the land of promise lies before them, that Yahweh has promised it to their ancestors (*Dt* 1.5–8), that it is there for the taking, that they shall have to drive out the present occupants and destroy all signs of their religion (*Numbers* 33.50–56).

A PROSPECT SYMBOLIZING THEIR HIGHEST EXPECTATIONS

To the people in the desert such a land of milk and honey represented all they could wish for. Likewise to a people in Exile, yet to conquer anew the Land (for whom the Priestly writer composes, including his creation story in *Genesis* 1), and to a recently returned people for whom The Chronicler writes, the land of promise remained a most desirable prospect. In that long prayer/homily in *Nehemiah* all its attractions are outlined as if still to be sampled (9.21–25).

YET A LAND THAT WAS ALSO BARREN AND CRUEL

In fact, as we would expect today, that land proved to be at times disappointing and harsh. Particularly those who had to work it to survive found it could fail to measure up to its promise; *Joel* describes in graphic detail the failure of harvest, lack of pasture, starving cattle, withering crops and vines, and—ultimate scourge—a plague of locusts (1.1–4,11–12,17–20).

CONQUEST OF THE LAND INVOLVING DISPOSSESSION OF OTHERS

As *Deuteronomy* and *Numbers* have recounted above, the Lord bade the people enter the land of Canaan and dispossess the occupants. This the people succeeded in doing, and the success recurs frequently in our written tradition. The various composers (whether in *Joshua*, the classic text, or later accounts like *Neh* 9.8; *Pss* 135; 136) show the relish with which the removal of each Canaanite tribe or token king was celebrated.

SETTLEMENT BEING ACHIEVED UNDER JOSHUA

Though the Old Testament generally is strangely silent about him, Joshua is given credit in the Deuteronomist's history for carrying out the entry into the Land, dispossessing the Canaanites, and allotting parcels of land to the tribes (*Jos* 24). Late in Old Testament times Ben Sira lists him as both general and prophet (*Sir* 46.1–8).

EACH TRIBE GOING TO ITS OWN TERRITORY

For the Deuteronomistic history completed six hundred years later, the division of Canaan was done simply enough by allotting land east and west of the Jordan as if no relics of other peoples remained. *Joshua*, having first described the conquest, sets about describing the allottment (13.1–7), also as if the tribes constituted a clear group of successors to the patriarchs to whom the land had been promised.

AS A REWARD FOR FIDELITY

Later theologizing by the Old Testament composers also stresses from their vantage point the granting of the Land as conditional upon the people's fidelity—a condition the composers know was not preserved, as the Land also was lost. The Priestly composer of *Leviticus* (in Exile) lectures his listeners on this need for fidelity (26.3–13). This too is the message of Joshua in the covenant rededication that closes the book (*Jos* 24.14–24) as the people prepare to settle down in comfort.

DISPOSSESSION OF THE LAND IN EXILE: THE ULTIMATE DISASTER

The cruel irony of the punishment for the people's infidelity—loss of the Land—was not lost on the prophets. Ezekiel, in exile with them in Babylon, taunts the people by reminding them of the promise of the Land to Abraham (rare in the prophets) and its fulfilment even in his lifetime, whereas the Land is now desolate (*Ez* 33.23–29).

A SIGN OF COMPLETE DIVINE DISPLEASURE

Those who write the people's history from the vantage point of Exile or return can in hindsight depict the Lord warning them severely of just this fate as a gauge of their God's displeasure for their infidelity, as the Priestly composer does in *Lev* 26.27–34. The Chronicler too, in that long piece of point-counterpoint in chapter 9 of *Nehemiah*, contrasting divine fidelity with the people's infidelity, reads them a stern lesson: "Here we are, slaves to this day—slaves in the land that you gave to our ancestors" (9.32–37).

REQUIRING A NEW EXODUS AND WILDERNESS EXPERIENCE

The only hope for these dispossessed people is the hope of those who first experienced enslavement and homelessness: intervention by the Lord, leading them out of captivity in a new Exodus and into the wilderness again preparatory to taking possession once more of the Land of promise. Second Isaiah promises the exiles just this (*Is* 43.16–21).

AND A NEW CONQUEST OF THE LAND

The Land was on the mind of the exiles as much as those in original captivity. The Priestly author, for whom conquest has never taken place, has this as his principal theme: in *Leviticus* the Lord promises (nominally the people in the desert, but in effect) the exiles yet to return that conquest is possible again (26.40–45). The condition of this reconquest, of course, is repentance (the Hebrew word is *shub*, "turn, return"). Ezekiel reminds the exiles of this (*Ez* 20.33–38), detailing the new distribution of the Land to the tribes on the model of Joshua's (*Ez* 47.21–48.7).

BUT THE LAND OF PROMISE LAY EVER AHEAD

After conquest, dispossession and reconquest—and so many other tribulations—it is small wonder that a less material, more mystical appreciation of the historical traditions provided a longer perspective. For the psalmist the true homeland lay elsewhere; we are foreigners here, "an alien, like all my forebears" (*Ps* 39.12; cf. 119.19). But the Old Testament generally cannot see far enough to discern that heavenly home.

Further reading
J. J. Schmitt, "The Land is mine," *TBT* 29 (1991 No. 6), 336–40
S. Pace Jeansonne, "The Land of Canaan," *TBT* 31 (1993 No. 3), 150–54
W. Brueggemann, *The Land*, Philadelphia: Fortress, 1977

EXERCISES

1. It is unusual to find an Old Testament book named after a woman. What does the book of *Ruth* say of woman's role in Israelite society of the time? Would you say the book is accurately titled?

2. Cast your mind back over the Old Testament books we have looked at so far, and list the cultural aspects found there that differ from our own. How far is that an obstacle to a full appreciation of the authors' message?

3. How far can you appreciate the Old Testament authors' obsession with the Land? Does that obsession throw light on contemporary events in Israel?

4. In Hebrew *nabi*, "prophet," means spokesperson, seer. Does Joel show us something of the role of a prophet in Israel?

CHAPTER 6

▼

RECORDING PAST AND PRESENT

texts: *1 Kings* **1–2 and** *1 Chronicles* **28–29;** *Genesis* **1–3**
biblical topic: Old Testament historical composition
theological theme: covenant, relationship, Law

One of the concerns, but by no means the sole concern, of biblical composers, orally and in writing, is to tell a story. The story they tell is, predictably, their own story, their people's history, where they have come from, what happened and why it happened—as far as they would like it to be seen. They are not overly concerned to give much attention or do justice to other peoples.

It is significant, as we have seen, that the Hebrew Bible refers to its commentators on past and present as *prophets*. The classic grouping of them as Historical Books in the Christian Bible is less accurate; it suggests that our modern, western style of *history* is involved and conceals their role of prophetic commentary (the Hebrew *nabi* implying spokesperson, commentator rather than seer). So the viewpoint of these composers is *theological* rather than *historical* in our sense: they endeavor to discern divine purposes in events.

In other words, the question we should address to the text of the Old Testament "historians" is not "what actually happened?" but "what significance should we find in the story?" (This is true of the New Testament as well.) The composers are interested primarily in the latter; it is *truth* they are after, not so much *facts* (which may not be available, or appropriate). Perhaps we flatter ourselves that in our time the reverse is the case; yet many a contemporary historian could agree with Australian biographer Alan Marshall, "I try to get beyond the facts to the truth." Think of cases where an assemblage of facts has concealed the truth!

1 Kings **1–2 and** *1 Chronicles* **28–29**

1) Whereas in our Christian Bible we find these two works among the Historical Books (see table, p. 10), the Hebrew Bible admits only the

73

former to the *Prophets*. That implies The Chronicler's work is not prophetic in the same way as that of The Deuteronomist (responsible for *Joshua* to *2 Kings*). Or it suggests—because it is a later work, or because it retells the earlier story—it could be classed as "leftovers" (*Paraleipomena*, as the LXX called the four books from *1 Chr* to *Neh*). Certainly both passages tell the same story, about the way Solomon acceded to the throne after David, but the composers have different interpretations of the accession. In the version of The Chronicler, dignity characterizes everything: David is a lordly figure in his demeanor, speaking and praying; Solomon is clearly chosen by the Lord and by David without mention of competitors, the building of the Temple is his first and greatest responsibility. By comparison The Deuteronomist's version in *Kings* is "warts and all"; the accession is by no means simple and dignified, but marked by intrigue, treachery and blood-letting. David is only a shadow of his former self; Solomon wins out, but only after plots and counterplots, and eventually has blood on his hands. No models here, as in the later version.

2) Let us consider further the dating and purposes of the two composers. The Deuteronomist is working at the time of Judah's fall, and is anxious to supply a theological basis for it; so negatives abound in his reworking of the records he cites, and no attempt is made to idealize the principal characters. David is paying for his sins, accession is achieved not by divine choice but by very human intrigue and bloodshed, Solomon is himself ruthless in eliminating opponents. All David can do for his son is to urge the fidelity he had not himself achieved. No mention of Temple and worship.

For The Chronicler, on the other hand, all is sweetness and light, and worship is a primary concern—as befits a composer endeavoring to supply a restored community with a model of life. No point in a composer of the fifth century or so offering a tainted dynasty as a model of a theocracy. So the well-known account is idealized, and Temple worship is central. It is suggested The Chronicler was a levite cantor.

3) In reading the passages again, we are awake to the different nuances of the two redactors and their theological purposes. We see the modification history takes at their hands in their different situations. While understanding why The Chronicler's work in the Hebrew Bible could be relegated to the Writings, we wonder if his version is any less *prophetic* in the biblical sense than The Deuteronomist's. Is history writing in our times utterly factual, dispassionate, or do historians leave us also with something of personal interpretation?

Further reading
T. P. Wahl, "*Chronicles*: the rewriting of history," *TBT* 26 (1988 No. 4), 197–202
C. Conroy, *1–2 Samuel, 1–2 Kings* (*OTM* 6)
C. Mangan, *1–2 Chronicles et al.* (*OTM* 13)

Genesis 1–3

1) Everyone knows these chapters from the opening of the Torah, or Pentateuch; but how many of us understand what the composers are trying to tell us? There are clearly two attempts here to do what many peoples and literatures have done, give an account of the origin (Greek *genesis*) of the world, or cosmogony; not all such are original, and we suspect these biblical ones are indebted to others in the cultural stream from which Old Testament composers drew. They are quite different: one is very ordered, pyramidal in development, reaching a climax in the creation of human beings and then the sabbath rest—an obviously religious motif; the other—beginning with the introductory phrase "These are the generations . . . "(2.4a)—sets a more circular scene, outlining an environment for the man and the woman, the limitations God sets for them and (in ch. 3) their failure to respect them under the influence of a figurative tempter. Nothing specifically nationalistic about either narrative: just the goodness of creation generally and the folly of human disobedience. If the second story aims to sketch human history before the patriarchs launch Israel's history, the first takes even that back further to cosmic history.

2) This is a book where we particularly need help from a range of critical resources: archeology, oriental literatures, literary criticism, language studies. They tell us that we are dealing with two different composers in the main. The Yahwist is so named for his use of *Yahweh* as a divine name, but with other characteristics as well—see Appendix 3, "Pentateuchal criticism". He is responsible for the second creation account and the whole theological movement that links patriarchs (from ch. 12) back to human origins and Fall. The Priestly composer supplies the later account in chapter 1, stressing order and goodness and hierarchy of existence, if not telling such a good story. Introductions tell us also of the resemblance to Mesopotamian creation stories, as well as the differences: God is in serene control, there is no conflict of chaotic forces. Women's later subordinate position in Israelite society is shown to be not original but the result of sin. Punishment of sin by death still leaves the way open to grace and hope.

3) We read the two accounts in these chapters again with a fresh

appreciation of what is going on—not just quaint cosmogonies but deliberate attempts to anchor Israel's later patriarchal and covenantal history on "two mighty theological pillars," as the great German commentator Gerhard Von Rad called the Priestly and Yahwistic creation narratives. We can see how simplistic and in fact erroneous it would be to look for a scientific version of creation here, as fundamentalists (such as creationists) do. A literalist interpretation of *Genesis* 3 would also not be a good basis for developing a theology of original sin, though Augustine and Thomas Aquinas in biblically less enlightened times would do that. It is interesting that nowhere else in the Old Testament will we find a prophet, psalmist or historian referring to the story of the Fall. Both narratives look forward to the beginning of Israel's own story in chapter 12, and should be read in that light.

Further reading

G. Von Rad, *Genesis (OTL)*, rev edn, ET London: SCM, 1972, chs 1&2

S. Greenhalgh, "*Genesis*, the narratives and the book," *Scripture Bulletin* 17 (1987 No. 2) 36–42

R. J. Clifford, "*Genesis* 1–3: permission to exploit nature?" *TBT* 26 (1988 No. 3) 133–37

H. P. Santmire, "The *Genesis* creation narratives revisited," *Int* 45 (1991 No. 4) 366–79

BIBLICAL TOPIC: OLD TESTAMENT HISTORICAL COMPOSITION

Our readings have made clear that "historical" has to be applied to our texts with many reservations; the Hebrew Bible, we have noted, avoids the term. The distance from modern, western style history is considerable, even if this too can be interpretative in function and not completely non-committal. Only fundamentalists will not allow the gap between the two styles, and will insist on taking accounts at face value. In recording past and present, the biblical composers generally prefer theological truth to historical fact (not always available); we should look for the particular truth intended in any text.

Primeval history

Accessibility to the facts is least evident in the primeval history of the first eleven chapters of *Genesis*. In place of fact about the world's origins the composers had available to them traditions and accounts of other peoples as well as etiologies and sagas explaining the significance of local places and figures. Israel's sages, interested in the age-old choice between good and evil, also made their contribution. What the three major composers of the primeval history did was to provide a theological thread linking Israel's story beginning with the patriarchal history back to the origins of all peoples and to accentuate truth about those origins—truth about God; truth about the human being and the world as the work of God's hands; about the goodness of things; about sin and its effect on people and things; about the action of grace and hope for the future. It is theology we are reading rather than history in our sense.

Patriarchal history

This theological accent continued in the composers who put together the patriarchal history (*Gn* 12–50). Working many centuries after the events they recounted, they incorporated ancient traditions, genealogies, etc., in such a way as to bring out certain themes: the blessing that would fall first on Abraham's descendants and through them on all humankind (Yahwist), the fear of God (Elohist), the need to fill the earth and subdue it (Priestly). Their message was influenced by the times in which they "wrote"; the Priestly editor of the Torah, for instance, perhaps working during the Exile, wanted to stress that conquest of the Land had now to be done all over again, so he omitted the first conquest.

Deuteronomist and Chronicler

Two great historians, or groups of historians, were responsible for composing or at least editing the story from settlement to monarchy and on to Exile, and from Exile to return and re-settlement: The Deuteronomist and The Chronicler. We have seen them above acting as theologians as much as historians, shaping traditional material to highlight their own theological message. Hence in the Hebrew Bible the work of The Deuteronomist is placed among the "Prophets", his prophetic message being that the word of the Lord always takes effect:

> "You promised with your mouth and have this day fulfilled with your hand,"

says Solomon at the dedication of the Temple in Jerusalem (*1 Kgs* 8.24). The Chronicler, responsible for (at least a degree of) editing of *1&2 Chronicles*, *Ezra* and *Nehemiah*, gives an idealised picture of the Davidic monarchy and Temple worship as the model for the life of the community returning to Jerusalem from Exile.

In short, these "historians" are working in the light of faith; they are thus theologians more than recorders. As J. L. McKenzie says, "In the Yahwist, as in the entire Old Testament, the acceptance of history as the execution of the designs of Yahweh demands an act of faith" (*NJBC* 1303). This theological viewpoint of theirs means the Bible gives us rather salvation history, where the emphasis and selection is determined by relevance to the welfare of the People. This differs from Bible history, where the

The Deuteronomistic History

The Hebrew Bible groups together as the Former Prophets the material (divided into "books" at a late stage) from *Joshua* to *2 Kings*. We recognize in all this material, beyond the ancient traditions involved and the sources cited, the controlling hand of a/some composer(s) intervening at a late moment to select/organize/adapt/ supplement the material from a particular viewpoint. Because of resemblances to the book of *Deuteronomy*, this hand is called that of a Deuteronomist (Dtr).

We have seen that this viewpoint is theological ("prophetic"), highlighting from the vantage point of the Exile (at least in its final form) the reasons for the disaster that has befallen: the people's infidelity to the covenant, and the efficacy of the word of the Lord.

We saw the hand of The Deuteronomist in the messy story of Solomon's accession; see also *1 Sam* 8 (on the ways of kingship), *2 Kgs* 17 (on the fall of the north).

The Chronicler's History

The Hebrew Bible contains a further corpus of "historical" com-position (in addition to Torah and Dtr), the books from *1 Chronicles* to *Nehemiah*. They are a late addition; the fact that they occur in The Writings, are not listed as prophets, and in fact occur in the Hebrew Bible in the order *Ezra, Nehemiah, Chronicles* suggests they were not given high priority. The LXX calls them "leftovers", *paraleipomena*.

Yet they too reveal a distinct theological viewpoint operating. It is perhaps not so much prophetic as regal and levitical, for its emphasis is very much on the Davidic monarchy and Temple worship as the model for the life of the restored community returned to Jerusalem after Exile.

The situation and purpose of The Chronicler is therefore differ-ent from Dtr. It seems the work of editing the similar material available to Dtr was completed by The Chronicler in the late fifth century (or later). Some would see less influence of the one editor in *Ezra* and *Nehemiah*.

emphasis falls instead on the spectacular (an accent visible also in Bible movies!), highlighting figures like Samson and Goliath, not so important in salvation history. Both obviously differ from ordinary secular reporting.

Further reading

A. F. Campbell, *The Study Companion to Old Testament Literature*, Wilmington: Glazier, 1989

J. R. Porter, "Old Testament historiography," *Tradition and Interpretation*, 125–62

R. K. Gnuse, "Holy history in the Hebrew Scriptures and the ancient world," *BTB* 17 (1987 No. 4) 127–36

P. R. Ackroyd, "The historical literature," *The Hebrew Bible and its Modern Interpreters*, 297–324

THEOLOGICAL THEME: COVENANT, RELATIONSHIP, LAW

(Be sure to read—aloud if possible—the passages nominated below.)

THE LORD CHOSE THE PEOPLE

Whatever connotations of political convenience are conveyed by the notion of covenant, treaty, alliance, "testament" (cf. "What's in a name?" p.187) used as a figure for the relationship between Yahweh and the chosen people, the Old Testament is convinced it rests on God's movement of love. "I have redeemed you, I have called you by name, you are mine," is the assurance given the exiles (*Isaiah* 43.1–4). *Deuteronomy* repeats that the relationship arises from God's love, not any virtue of the people (7.6–10).

RELATING THEM TO HIMSELF BY COVENANT ON SINAI

The narrative of the epiphany in the wilderness of Sinai in *Exodus* shows God stressing both redemptive intervention on the people's behalf—bearing them up on eagles' wings—and the willingness to make them the "treasured possession out of all the peoples" (19.3–6). Hosea will translate this into the imagery of marriage: "I will take you for my wife in faithfulness," says the Lord, harking back to that time (*Hos* 2.14–20).

THE RELATIONSHIP WAS BASED ON THE LORD'S OWN INITIATIVE

So the covenant as a whole, and all the stipulations of the Law, come from the Lord's initiative; the Torah stresses this in introducing it both in *Exodus* and again in *Deuteronomy* 5.1–7. The prophets like to remind the people of this, too, like Ezekiel in his allegory of the orphan found and raised by a doting parent (*Ez* 16.1–8).

BUT REQUIRING RESPONSE AND FIDELITY FROM THEM

Torah and Prophets alike insist as well that the relationship, the marriage is bilateral, conditional upon the people's response and fidelity. The Jewish prayer *Shemah*, which incorporates part of the text of *Deuteronomy* 6.1–9, daily reminds one of the need for total love in return. The prophet Micah in the eighth century will specify this response: "To do justice, and to love kindness, and to walk humbly with your God" (*Mic* 6.6–8).

THEIR RESPONSE WAS OUTLINED IN THE LAW OF MOSES

In greater detail than Micah and in more legal terms than images of marriage and adoption, the response was detailed in the Book of the Covenant in the Torah. In the manner of such covenants the people signified their commitment in blood in a ceremonial that Moses solemnized (*Exodus* 24.3–8). The later account of the Sinai covenant in *Nehemiah* 9.12–14 is also in terms of laws, statutes and commandments.

WHICH CONTAINED ALL MORALITY AND WISDOM

The Law thus became the compendium of Israel's way of life (explaining our simplistic identification of "Torah" and "Law"). All the 176 verses of *Psalm* 119 exalt the virtues of laws/statutes/ordinances/precepts . . . Israel's Wisdom literature in its most pious statements will see all wisdom encapsulated in the Mosaic Law (*Sirach* 24.23–27).

BUT THE PEOPLE WERE NOT FAITHFUL TO THE LAW

The overriding message of Israel's prophetic literature is that such fidelity was not forthcoming. Jeremiah, seeing impending doom, accuses the people of forgetting the commitment they made in the wilderness (*Jer* 7.21–26). The Chronicler, from the vantage point of post-exilic times, produces that great survey of Israel's history based on the themes of divine fidelity/national infidelity (*Neh* 9.26).

AND EVEN MADE A MOCKERY OF IT

The worst attitude to the covenant, in Jeremiah's view, was not simply the people's non-compliance with it (he lists particular prescriptions they have violated: 7.5–9), but their recital of pious catchcries at the same time (7.1–4). Such hypocrisy made repentance impossible.

THEY WERE PUNISHED FOR THEIR INFIDELITY

So the prophets and historians took satisfaction in chronicling the appropriate fate of such covenant infidelity. To The Deuteronomist the fall of both north (*2 Kgs* 17.7–18) and south are occasions for observing, "This occurred because the people had sinned against the Lord their God." The Chronicler, too, labors the same reason for the fact that "we are slaves to this day" (*Neh* 9.32–37).

THEY REPENTED AND RETURNED TO OBSERVANCE OF THE LAW

The way to a restored relationship and relief from suffering was likewise obvious: renewed observance of the Law. To both these historians the figure of King Josiah stands out in the late seventh century for his spirited attempt to promote such observance once "the book of the Law" (perhaps a copy of *Deuteronomy*) was discovered (*2 Chr* 34.29–33).

BUT A NEW, INTERIOR RELATIONSHIP WOULD BE REQUIRED

There were those, however, who saw that a new relationship would be required, something interior that would be proof against externalizing and lip-service. In "one of the profoundest and most moving passages of the entire Bible" (John Bright), Jeremiah looks forward to a new covenant (testament) in days to come, a new law written on people's hearts, not in stone or books (*Jer* 31.31–34—the longest Old Testament quotation in the New Testament). In a similar vein, but with his own accents on divine holiness, Ezekiel forecasts the granting of a new spirit and a heart of flesh if the people are to become God's people again (*Ez* 36.23–28). Hence the New Testament usage of speaking of a new covenant/testament.

Further reading
S. Terrien, *The Elusive Presence*, 106–160
S. D. McBride, "Transcendent authority: the role of Moses in Old Testament traditions," *Int* 44 (1990 No. 3) 229–39
P. D. Miller, "The place of the Decalogue in the Old Testament and its laws," *Int* 43 (1989 No. 3) 229–42

EXERCISES

1. Can you see the difference between prophetical history, as in The Deuteronomist, and modern, western historiography? Think of some recent history writing that bears the marks of interpretation and comment as well as factual record.
2. Make a close comparison of the two versions of Solomon's accession. Why does each take the form it does?
3. Make a similar comparison of the two creation stories in *Genesis* 1–2. Also, how significant do you find it that the story of the Fall does not dominate Old Testament thinking in the way it does Christian theology?
4. Can you see what is concealed in the unfortunate Latin term (Old/New) "testament"? Are you able to bring out the full significance of the ideas of covenant, relationship, law?

CHAPTER 7

VARIETY IN ENFLESHING THE WORD

texts: *Nehemiah 8–9; Sirach 44–46*
biblical topic: Old Testament literary types
theological theme: sin, repentance, return

If our task in reading the Scriptures that Jesus knew is to meet the Word enfleshed there, we must be prepared to meet him in various guises—just as people in later times had to recognize him variously enfleshed as the babe of Bethlehem, the prophet from Nazareth, the man of sorrows. We are justified in making that parallel, as biblical commentators have made it from the earliest times of Christianity. One of those great early commentators, John Chrysostom, preacher in Antioch and later patriarch of Constantinople, is cited by the Second Vatican Council for this insight in its statement on the Bible:

> *The words of God, expressed in human languages, became like human discourse,*
> JUST AS *of old*
> *the Word of the eternal Father, taking flesh of our human limitations, became like human beings (*Dei Verbum *13).*

Acceptance of that principle helps us avoid pitfalls into which both fundamentalists and scholars have fallen in approaching the Old Testament. The former want to find there only historical record of the type to which they are accustomed; hence they may come to our doors promoting a creationist viewpoint on the basis of a superficial reading of *Genesis*, or may wish to explain *Daniel* or some other apocalyptic text as a precise statement of present or coming events. Scholars, while aware of such differences in biblical material, have at times given almost exclusive attention to one type, such as historical traditions, neglecting lyrical and sapiential (Wisdom) composition, as though these were deficient in not dealing with Israel's story. Our task is to recognize the Word enfleshed in a variety of forms and genres.

Prophets and priests, poets and peasants, sages and seers, sinners and saints, cantors and kings, levites and lawyers, psalmists and preachers—all have in their own individual styles mediated the Word to us in the Old Testament. For that variety we are grateful.

Nehemiah 8–9

1) In pondering basic theological themes above that are basic to the Old Testament, we have several times quoted from the long prayer/homily in these chapters of *Nehemiah*. We are reading from the third "historical" corpus of the Hebrew Bible that is found there among The Writings, and among the Historical Books in the Christian Bible, and that is thought to some degree to fall under the influence of The Chronicler. It tells of the exiles' life in Jerusalem on return, guided by Nehemiah the governor and Ezra the priest and scribe, with a particular role for the levites; the precise dating is vague. Chapter 8 describes a public reading by Ezra of some part of the Mosaic Law, which reduces the people to tears. This is followed by celebration of the festival of Booths. Chapter 9 proceeds to another festival, like the Day of Atonement, *Yom Kippur* (with some concern about the presence of foreigners, v. 2), then the long prayer/homily recited by levites or (in LXX) Ezra, surveying the whole of Israel's salvation history on a point-counterpoint pattern highlighting divine fidelity-Israel's infidelity. We have seen the pattern before in cultic credos; the rhythms strike us as deuteronomic.

2) Reference to scholarship confirms our uncertainty about chronology and the placing of these chapters in the whole corpus ascribed to The Chronicler. It seems to be the late fifth century that is being described. These chapters suddenly terminate slabs of genealogies dear to The Chronicler with his cultic interests; perhaps the chapters have been rearranged at some stage. The chronicling of events is very close, whereas the scope of the survey in the prayer is vast. Contamination of the community was an issue for the returned.

3) A re-reading allows us to savor the emphases of the composer(s). The Law is important for this community, and especially liturgical celebration of festivals (prescribed in the reading of *Leviticus*?). Covenant fidelity is critical for them: the prayer is based completely on that theme. Thus, in one brief passage we are treated to the microscopic reporting of an historical monograph, complete with precise (if unclear) time references and long lists of names, and also to a vast sweep of salvation history in the form of a prayer or homily.

Further reading
J. M. Myers, *Ezra, Nehemiah (AB 14)*

S. Talmon, "*Ezra* and *Nehemiah*" in R. Alter, F. Kermode, *The Literary Guide to the Bible*, London: Fontana, 1989, 357–64

Sirach 44–46

1) This book, which is also called *Ecclesiasticus* ("churchy") in some versions, is one of the deuterocanonical books not finally accepted by the rabbis after Jesus' time, and is a Wisdom book. So it is quite different biblical material from the *Nehemiah* we have just read, though it too conducts a sweeping survey of history in our chapters, the beginning of a "Hymn in honour of our ancestors." The difference in this survey is that the characters chosen for mention are heroes not only of Israel but go back beyond Abraham to Enoch and Noah—universal forebears of the whole human race. A further difference of the survey is that the basis of the selection of generally human and specifically Israelite figures is the gift of wisdom they exemplify, not military or political prowess. These differences remind us of the wide perspective of Wisdom material—in Israel and beyond (see Appendix 4). We recognize the text, especially the opening verses of chapter 44, as one used often in panegyrics (it could be used only of males, no women rating a mention—as we observed above in speaking of the position of women in chapter 5). The book's opening explains that the work was composed in Hebrew by a Ben Sira (*Sirach* being a Greek form) and translated into Greek by his grandson in Egypt around 132 or later; so the original must come from early that century.

2) Hebrew manuscripts of the book have only recently been found; so the rabbis would not have taken kindly to the language of translation, the Egyptian connection, the patently late date (though in fact earlier than some canonical books, like *Daniel*), the lack of affirmation of life after death (see *canon* above, p.38). Yet the book is a favorite with the New Testament (and presumably Jesus, who is found quoting it: cf. *Mt* 11.28–30), some rabbis and early Church Fathers. It gives us the earliest evidence that sages like Ben Sira ran schools of Wisdom in Israel; this book may be his notes for his pupils.

3) In re-reading the chapters we appreciate the sapiential (Wisdom) outlook of Ben Sira who could both relish his nation's history and yet see the relevance of non-Israelite members of the human race, to whom also God gave the gift of wisdom. He is clearly proud of the religious traditions of his people, superior to Hellenistic ways; for him the pre-eminent codification of wisdom is the Law. This hymn, both in its hymnic form and its historical sweep, differs from the normal brief *meshalim*, proverbs, of earlier Wisdom. What a pity that decisions

reached in the heat of controversy, both among pharisaic Judaism and at the Reformation, have discouraged people from reading this excellent vehicle of the Word. Jesus knew and loved it.

Further reading

P. W. Skehan, A. Di Lella, *The Wisdom of Ben Sira* (*AB* 39)

W. Roth, "*Sirach*: the first graded curriculum," *TBT* 29 (1991 No. 5), 298–302

R. C. Hill, *Jesus and the Mystery of Christ*, Melbourne: Collins Dove, 1993, 59–61

BIBLICAL TOPIC: OLD TESTAMENT LITERARY TYPES

Only fundamentalists would ignore the evidence of the rich literary diversity of the Old Testament—much more varied than the New Testament (which can be said to have compensating features, of course). This *variety of forms, types, genres* offers challenge as well as richness: we need to study the material to recognize the particular form being employed by psalmist or sage or annalist. Vatican II urged scholars to just this work of recognition:

> *Truth is proposed and expressed in a variety of ways, depending on whether a text is history of one kind or another, or whether its form is that of prophecy, poetry or some other type of speech* (Dei Verbum 12).

Biblical scholars have long accepted the further element of challenge in determining the literary nature of the material by first accepting the complexity of authorship of Old Testament material. Owing to the long tradition of pre-existing material, the final shape of a text includes the work of many contributors in forms that once had independent existence. Form criticism unearths these pre-existing forms in a now deceptively uniform text (see chapter 4 on "biblical criticism").

"History"

Old Testament "history", for instance, involves a spectrum of material, from primeval history (*Gn* 1–11) and patriarchal stories (*Gn* 12–50) to later traditions. The older traditions incorporate creation epics, etiological sagas and genealogies aimed at legitimizing the existence of towns like Mamre and Bethel (*Gn* 18 & 28), epics from other cultures (the flood stories of *Gn* 6–9), cultic credos (*Dt, Jos*), fables (*Nm* 22), covenant formulas and laws (*Ex, Dt*). The more recent historical compositions of The

Deuteronomist and The Chronicler—as much theology as history—also include pre-existing forms such as psalms (*2 Sam* 22), prophetic oracles (*2 Sam* 12.7ff.), parables (*2 Sam* 12.1–4), annunciations (*Jgs* 13.2–5). All these make for history with a difference—something fundamentalists ignore.

Prophecy

The prophetical books of the Old Testament also have a lengthy and complicated history of composition, and now incorporate a range of pre-existing forms in a finally edited sequence, basically the prophetic oracles of various kinds but also others:

visions	messenger formulas
symbolic actions	promises
war oracles	threats
invectives	admonitions
reproaches	warnings
private oracles	hymns
liturgies	laments
allegories	

Wisdom

The Old Testament Wisdom literature, too, has generally passed through stages of composition. *Sirach*, coming from Ben Sira's own hand into his grandson's, would be an exception. Its basic form is the *mashal*, proverb, but a range of other forms have lately been recognized there (in today's "pan-sapiential" climate, a reaction against previous neglect of Wisdom—and equally extreme?):

numerical formulae	didactic narratives
riddles	hymns
parables	laws
fables	torah
allegories	exhortations
disputations	woe oracles
autobiographical narratives	psalms

Elsewhere in the Old Testament we can recognize this variety of type and assimilation of pre-existing forms into one text, like *Song of Songs*. *Ruth* has been inserted into the Deuteronomist's history as a genealogical and juridical footnote on David's ancestry and remarriage customs. *Tobit, Judith* and *Esther* represent that type of rabbinic commentary on Scripture known as *midrash*, bringing out a religious message (see Appendix 2, "Word and text; rabbis; Talmud"). *Jonah* is similarly midrashic, an historical novel composed for prophetical purposes.

The New Testament will use a neologism to describe God's grand design for humankind and the cosmos: *polypoikilos* (*Ephesians* 3.10), which the *NRSV* will nicely turn as "of a rich variety," picking up the twofold idea of a cloth that is multicolored and finely textured. That rich variety, which we owe to the "creator of all things" (*Eph* 3.9), is equally evident and equally generous in the Word that comes to us in the Scriptures known to Jesus, who himself would employ a range of such forms of expression.

Further reading
M. Trainor, *Befriending the Text*, Melbourne: Collins Dove, 1991
D. J. Harrington, "Form criticism," *Interpreting the Old Testament*, 69–82
R. E. Murphy, "Pentateuchal literary forms," *NJBC* 5–6

THEOLOGICAL THEME: SIN, REPENTANCE, RETURN

(Be sure to read—aloud if possible—the passages nominated below.)

THE GOD OF ISRAEL IS A HOLY, LOVING AND COMPASSIONATE GOD

There are no real grounds in the Old Testament for thinking Israel's God is simply vindictive. Instead, Torah and prophets (at least) are insistent that their God is loving by nature and loving in their regard. To Hosea God is like a loving parent trying time after time to lift a (sometimes froward) child to his cheek (*Hos* 11.1–4), "the Holy One in your midst, who will not come in wrath" (11.9).

WHOSE LOVING-KINDNESS TO ISRAEL DEMANDS RESPONSE IN FIDELITY

The relationship between Yahweh and Israel that is worked out in covenant terms is, like any proper relationship, dependent on a response to gratuitous beneficence on God's part. We have seen that a proper understanding of "Ten Commandments" implies as much (ch. 3 above). So *Deuteronomy* proceeds at once from covenant love to observance of commandments, statutes, ordinances (7.7–12).

SO THE NATION'S WORST SIN IS COVENANT INFIDELITY

In this context sin above all is infidelity to the requirements of the relationship binding the people to their loving God. A prophet-historian like The Deuteronomist has no difficulty diagnosing the root cause of national disaster as grievous sin of this kind: despite warnings both north and south "despised his statutes and his covenant that he made with their ancestors", and suffered for it (*2 Kings* 17.13–17).

A SIN WHICH IS LIKE INFIDELITY IN MARRIAGE

From the other side of approaching disaster Hosea sees northern infidelity in less legalistic, more intimate terms as a bride's infidelity to her husband: she has played the whore, and her children are the children of whoredom (*Hos* 2.1–5). There is no question as to the horror of the national sin.

AND WHICH BESMIRCHES THE HOLINESS OF GOD

It is the prophets of the Exile, Jeremiah and Ezekiel, who protest about the holiness of God being compromised by covenant infidelities—abominations, adulteries, prostitutions (*Jer* 13.27). Ezekiel, with his interest in the cult and his affinity with the Holiness Code of *Leviticus*, accuses Judah of profaning God's holy name among the nations (*Ez* 36.22–23).

AND INEVITABLY INCURS PUNISHMENT BY THE GOD OF THE COVENANT

Prophets like Jeremiah who unsuccessfully strove to get the people to return to observance of the covenant eventually had to concede that they had failed and that punishment lay ahead (*Jer* 14.17–18). From a later vantage point historian-theologians would labor the inevitability of such punishment due both to popular infidelity and to the irretractability of the Word of Lord; The Deuteronomist says as much in commenting on the fall of Judah (*2 Kgs* 17.19–23).

THOUGH GOD'S COVENANT LOVE CONTINUES

To the biblical authors necessary punishment of infidelity does not mean God's departure from the initial promise. From the despair of the Babylonian sack of Jerusalem *Lamentations* appeals to the Lord to recall this promise of unfailing love (5.19–22). The *Psalms* also frequently remind worshippers of this truth (*Ps* 78.38).

TO THE SAGES IDOLATRY IS THE WORST SIN

The Wisdom composers, less attached to historical and covenantal tradition, and more alert to cosmic and universally human concerns, see the most heinous sin in replacement of (Israel's) God with idols—creatures replacing the creator (*Wisdom* 13.1–3).

ISRAEL CAME TO SEE THE INDIVIDUAL CHARACTER OF SIN

While much historical and prophetical thought is directed to the people's fidelity and infidelity and retribution for both, the Old Testament gradually awoke to personal and not merely social responsibility. Ezekiel breaks new ground here (*Ez* 18), dealing with the case of the good person who sins as well as the sinner turning away from sin.

WHICH ALSO NECESSARILY INCURS INDIVIDUAL PUNISHMENT

The corollary for Ezekiel is that individual sin incurs individual punishment, whereas age-old proverbs had suggested one suffers for one's parents' sins (*Jer* 31.29). *Deuteronomy*'s version of the Law had already upheld the principle (*Dt* 24.16), but Ezekiel in exile had to labor the point of the need of personal owning of the Torah by people who now had no clear country or community that would be collectively responsible.

SIN HAS COSMIC EFFECTS

While Old Testament thought is community centered—and one community at that—there is occasional acknowledgement that the whole cosmos is affected by human behavior. The *Genesis* story of the Fall (*Gn* 3) suggests as much. Prophets also can point to cosmic effects of sin (*Nahum* 1.2–5).

FORGIVENESS OF SIN INVOLVES CONVERSION, RETURN TO COVENANT OBSERVANCE

The God of the covenant is ever ready to forgive the people's departure from it - provided they "turn back" (Hebrew *shub*). To the Deuteronomist the paradigm is Josiah, who reversed the trend of his predecessors and "turned to the Lord with all his heart, with all his soul, and with all his might" (*2 Kgs* 23.24–25). Hosea tells the north there is no other way: "Return, O Israel, to the Lord your God" (*Hos* 14.1–3).

AND IS READILY ACCORDED BY A FORGIVING GOD

This is the consoling obverse of prophetic denunciation: the Lord will relent (*Amos* 7.2–3), sometimes even to the apparent disappointment of the prophet, as the book of *Jonah* highlights—God is too ready to forgive even the most evil of the nations if they repent (*Jonah* 4.10–11). Ready forgiveness is a constant theme in the *Psalms* (*Ps* 103.1–3).

Further reading

M. T. McHatten, "Turn from your wickedness," *TBT* 30 (1992 No. 2), 80–83

J. L. McKenzie, "Sin, forgiveness (in the Old Testament)," *NJBC* 1305–1307

J. Milgrom, "Repentance in the Old Testament," *IDB Supp* 736–38

EXERCISES

1. Read again that long sermon/prayer in chapter 9 of *Nehemiah*. Can you see how the author has patterned it to bring out the correlative themes of fidelity/infidelity?

2. Can you appreciate Ben Sira's purpose in drawing up that litany of Israel's heroes (of wisdom) in chapters 44–46, and how it differs from the list a Yahwist, Deuteronomist or Chronicler might construct?

3. Have you gained from your reading of the Old Testament so far a sense of its greater literary diversity by comparison with the New Testament? Compile a list of the literary types you have encountered.

4. Though the Fall may not be a constant theme in the Old Testament, there is no doubt of the emphasis on sin. In what various ways does it think of sin?

CHAPTER 8

DIVINE WORD,
HUMAN WORD

texts: *Ecclesiastes* 1–3; *Judges* 19
biblical topic: inspiration and biblical truth
theological theme: evil, suffering, retribution

Our purpose in reading the Old Testament is to meet and benefit from the Word of God in its pages. We are prepared and in fact compelled to bring to the task all the skills and resources human ingenuity has devised for literary appreciation generally; and yet we believe that, in the text, we are reading a divine Word. There is a paradox here, of course: the material is both human and divine in origin, and to discover the divine message we must attend to the human message.

The paradox is that of incarnation: in the human the divine has taken form. As we have emphasized from the outset, the scriptural incarnation occurs on the paradigm of the historical incarnation. We recognize in the human person of Jesus a divine statement, a divine Word; to interpret the latter we study the humanity in which it is graciously expressed for our more ready understanding. The earliest Christian commentators on the Bible acknowledged this gracious considerateness by the divine communicator of the Word. John Chrysostom, a great Eastern preacher of the fourth century, said of a passage of *Genesis* that seemed mundane: "Do you see God's considerateness (*synkatabasis*)? It is not with a view to his own dignity that he chooses his words but out of considerateness for our limitations."

There are passages in both testaments that make us wonder what divine truth is being expressed there, just as there are those people who find a first century Jewish male an unlikely savior. We accept from our Christian forebears that our Scriptures are inspired by God, unlikely as that may seem at times. Already in the New Testament this challenge had been faced. "You must understand this, that no prophecy of scripture is a matter of one's own interpretation, because no prophecy ever came by human will, but men and women moved by the Holy Spirit spoke from God" (*2 Peter* 1.20–21). We read Old Testament texts, mundane and elevating in turn, in this belief.

Ecclesiastes 1-3

1) Certainly in reading this quite dyspeptic commentator on daily life one wonders how "inspired" the material is. Anyone who teaches (the author is said to be a "preacher," *Qoheleth*—even Solomon?) that "there is nothing better for mortals than to eat and drink" has a dubious claim to divine inspiration, we feel, especially when he adds, "The fate of humans and the fate of animals is the same." For a piece of Wisdom literature, this book has no healthy regard for wisdom itself; it concludes that the same fate befalls fools and wise alike. It does admit that everything comes from the hand of God, but adds that it is futile— "vanity" is a constant motif—to try to change the pattern God has determined. There are set times for everything (how could we ever have enjoyed that poem in chapter 3?). The truth contained in the book seems much more human than divine, even if we can resonate (on a bad day!) with some of Qoheleth's reflections on people and things.

2) So we are not surprised to learn that the rabbis at Jamnia had doubts about including this book in the canon of the Hebrew Bible. It cannot be Solomon's work, to judge from the language (plenty of Aramaisms) and the radically sceptical tone. It is clearly a late composition, at a time when everything was up for question; the Qumran community knew it, so it is possibly to be dated in the third century. *Ecclesiastes* is the Greek form of Qoheleth—perhaps "preacher." Somebody has added a postscript to the book in the final half-dozen verses.

3) Read Appendix 4, "Biblical Wisdom." You will note that the sages generally claimed not divine inspiration but the value of human experience as the source of their teaching. They talk more of mundane realities than of worship, law, history. It is their strength rather than weakness to be in touch with the real world and people generally, rather than simply the Jewish people and religious realities. In this light we can read Qoheleth again and see a truth there: life, for all its disappointments (the lot of a great number of people, after all), is in God's hands—not so much the God of the patriarchs as a universal Providence. This is a far more realistic, "truthful", view of life than the highly idealized interpretation of some biblical history (e.g. The Chronicler) or apocalyptic. If we accept the scriptural incarnation, we cannot expect all the authors to be as mystical as Ezekiel or as consoling as Second Isaiah. (We recall that of *James* in the New Testament Luther said, "That epistle of straw"—and yet today we find its social sensitivity very relevant.)

Further reading
R. E. Murphy, "Qoheleth and theology?" *BTB* 21 (1991 No. 1), 30–33
M. Laumann, "Qoheleth and time," *TBT* 27 (1989 No. 5), 305–310
D. Bergant, *Job, Ecclesiastes* (*OTM* 18)

Judges 19

1) This is a hair-raising story by any standard. If the author is trying to show how lawless things were in the time of the judges "when there was no king in Israel" (v. 1), he certainly succeeds. In fact, he succeeds to a greater extent with modern readers than he could have imagined: we react to the treatment of the levite's concubine well before the point of her abuse by the men of Gibeah. Though the dismembering of her corpse at the end of the chapter precipitates a civil war that concludes the period of the judges, allowing prophets and kings to come on stage (in *1&2 Samuel*), we are already appalled by the way this woman is treated as a chattel by parent and "husband". She never says a word, not when the men are talking and drinking in her father's house for days on end nor when she is thrown to the mob as substitute victim. The levite shows no remorse for his action nor even sensitivity to her likely condition the morning after; he has no compunction about dispatching pieces of her corpse around Israel to settle scores. We wonder whether the truth of this "inspired" passage is identical with what the author intended to convey.

2) The material in this closing section of *Judges* lay outside the scope of The Deuteronomist's redaction of early traditions of the period of the twelfth and eleventh centuries, and was included later as an epilogue. It is interested in the plight of the landless levites and in Bethlehem, home of the future king David. Interaction between tribes and clans, villages and regions in this intermediary period of history (from Joshua to Saul) is also of interest to the final post-deuteronomistic compiler of traditions.

3) We can appreciate the purpose of the inclusion of this story by the Israelite historians; there is a truth to be learnt, and we can concede divine inspiration at work, despite its chilling effect. A feminist reading today will draw from it more than the author intended, an unsuspected truth—of the place of women in the society of the period. Deborah looms large as woman, prophet and judge in *Judges*, and yet Samson's mother and wife—key figures—are nameless, as is the levite's concubine. The author is not utterly insensitive to the oppression and savagery he records: note the pathetic phrase in v. 27, when the levite casually opens the door next morning to go on his way and finds his concubine

lying at the door of the house "with her hands on the threshold." An "inspired" touch?

Further reading

M. O'Connor, "*Judges*," *NJBC*

P. Trible, *Texts of Terror*, Philadelphia: Fortress, 1984, 65–91

V. H. Matthews, "Hospitality and hostility in *Genesis* 19 and *Judges* 19," *BTB* 22 (1992 No. 1), 3–12

BIBLICAL TOPIC: INSPIRATION AND BIBLICAL TRUTH

consequence

When we think of the obvious limitations of authors like Qoheleth and the composer of *Judges*, we wonder about the meaning and effect of scriptural inspiration. We are much more at ease with prophets and psalmists and sages of a more patently religious frame of mind. The Incarnation—unfortunately (?)—does not allow us to pick and choose the mediators of the Word; there may be an obtrusively large element of the human in what is conveyed at times when we might prefer simply the divine—just as any Arab might prefer a mediator who was not a Jew like Jesus. The Christian community accepts both human and divine involvement in our Scriptures in saying (as does Vatican II) that as a result of divine inspiration "they have God for their author and have been handed on as such to the Church herself."

> *In composing the sacred books God chose human beings and while employed by him they made use of their powers and abilities, so that with him acting in them and through them they, as true authors, consigned to writing everything and only those things which he wanted (Dei Verbum 11).*

Biblical truth

The purpose of the scriptural incarnation, as of the historical Incarnation, is the salvation of humankind. Hence the principal effect of biblical inspiration is the saving truth brought to us by the inspired Word. The kind of truth in any particular biblical text depends on the nature of the composition:

> *Truth is proposed and expressed in a variety of ways, depending on whether its form is that of prophecy, poetry, or some other type of speech. The interpreter must investigate what meaning the sacred writer intended to express and*

actually expressed in particular circumstances as he used contemporary literary forms in accordance with the situation of his own time and culture (ibid. 12).

We are thus discouraged from looking for statistical or scientific inerrancy in passages not so intended. The truth we are looking for is *biblical truth*, "that truth which God wanted put into the sacred writings for the sake of our salvation" (*Dei Verbum* 11). What that saving truth is in any particular passage we will have to work hard to discover. *Ecclesiastes* and *Judges* set us a challenge there; in the case of the latter we saw a double truth, "what meaning the sacred writer intended to express and actually expressed," as the Council says. Likewise, the first creation narrative in *Genesis* conveys a different truth from the second—but both are true in the sense of biblical truth, as each contains a truth (or truths) relevant to our salvation.

Fundamentalism

Fundamentalists fail to grasp the notion of biblical truth because they do not properly understand biblical inspiration (and, more basically, incarnation). They do not concede (with Vatican II) that truth takes different forms according to the types of writing; for them Jonah's adventures at sea are of the same kind of reporting as the rebuilding of Jerusalem's walls in *Nehemiah*. They also see inerrancy as the principal effect of inspiration, so no factual inaccuracy can be tolerated. This is tantamount to seeing Jesus' physical perfection as the principal purpose of the Incarnation, our salvation coming a poor second. In looking in the Bible for *fact* rather than *truth* they part company even with contemporary writers we have quoted like Alan Marshall, who claims, "I try to get beyond the facts to the truth," and John Mortimer (author of *Rumpole of the Bailey, Paradise Postponed* and other TV series), whose view is, "The greatest preoccupation of a writer is to tell the truth of some sort, as he sees it." The divine guidance that is biblical inspiration helped composers like Qoheleth achieve just that; we have to make our contribution by recognizing the truth contained in their work "for the sake of our salvation."

Further reading

L. Alonso Schökel, *The Inspired Word. Scripture in the Light of Language and Literature*, ET, New York: Herder and Herder, 1965

S. Brown, "New directions in biblical interpretation," *TBT* 27 (1989 No. 4), 197–202

THEOLOGICAL THEME: EVIL, SUFFERING, RETRIBUTION

(Be sure to read—aloud if possible—the passages nominated below.)

LIFE IN THIS WORLD INVOLVES US IN EVIL AND SUFFERING

The Old Testament's sapiential literature is particularly concerned with these realities, e.g. *Job*. Qoheleth, too, is depressed by "the evil deeds that are done under the sun" (*Eccl* 4.1–3). The primeval history in *Genesis* probes the origins of evil and suffering in the world, with assistance from other cultures' exploration of the problem.

THE EVIL OF SIN IS THE CAUSE OF THIS SUFFERING

With the exception of some radical questioning (as in *Job*), the Old Testament attributes suffering to sin. For the Yahwist it can all be traced back to the original departure from God's will in the garden, even down to thorns and thistles (*Gn* 3.17–19). As late as the second century the pious Ben Sira is repeating this formula, in an even more sexist version: "From a woman sin had its beginning, and because of her we all die" (*Sir* 25.24).

IN PARTICULAR, BREAKING GOD'S LAW RESULTS IN PUNISHMENT

For Torah and Prophets generally, sin has a covenantal dimension, as has punishment. There is a clear choice between observing statutes and commandments, with the consequent material benefits this entails, and disobedience and its consequences. So "choose life so that you and your descendants may live," says Deuteronomy (30.15–20).

IT IS THE PEOPLE WHO SIN, AND THE PEOPLE WHO SUFFER

To this mentality sin is social because the covenant binds the people to God and requires fidelity of them. Corporate responsibility is a major theme of The Deuteronomist in his attempt to review traditions in the light of impending disaster; it was all "the Israelites who did what was evil in the sight of the Lord" and suffered for it (*Jgs* 6.1–6). In the eighth century Isaiah is of the same mind about social injustice (*Is* 3.13–17).

BUT THE INDIVIDUAL CAN BE RESPONSIBLE

In opposition to the theological view that children suffered for parents' sins and vice versa (as in the case of Eli, *1 Sam* 3.10–14), there developed by the time of Jeremiah and Ezekiel the conviction that the Lord deals with father and son individually (*Ez* 18). The proverb, "The parents have eaten sour grapes, and the children's teeth are set on edge," is finally laid to rest.

ISRAEL'S HISTORY SHOWED THIS PATTERN OF SIN AND SUFFERING

Prophets Former and Latter took satisfaction in theologising on this theme in surveying the nation's history. The primary requirement of the covenant, fidelity to the one true God, was violated, from the days of the Judges to the eve of the Exile, and resulted in heavy punishment on the people. So says The Deuteronomist of the earlier period (*Jgs* 2.11–15), so says an oracle through Jeremiah of the latter (*Jer* 17.1–4).

THE EXILE REPRESENTED THE CLASSIC CASE OF PUNISHMENT FOR SIN

For such historian-theologians working from the vantage point of impending disaster for Judah in the sixth century, what was clearly about to ensue represented a *locus classicus* of which they took advantage. The Deuteronomist diagnoses the problem as national default as it had been in the case of the north (*2 Kgs* 17.1–20): "Judah also did not keep the commandments of the Lord their God but walked in the customs that Israel had introduced."

RELIEF DEPENDED ON CONFESSION AND REPENTANCE

Escape from punishment, national or personal, lay within reach if there was first a turning to the Lord: *shub*, return, is The Deuteronomist's constant exhortation, as also the moralist's platitude in the mouth of Zophar in *Job* (11.13–17), and the penitent's prayer of true remorse (*Ps* 51).

PROSPERITY INDICATED A GOOD LIFE BLESSED BY GOD

Moralists on this theme abound in the Old Testament's sapiential material, peddling the traditional equation of virtue and reward, sin and punishment. The book of *Proverbs* has countless such maxims (*Prv* 11.17–21), and Wisdom psalms dwell on the same theme (*Ps* 1).

THOUGH THE EQUATION CAME UNDER QUESTION

Perhaps in the wake of national disillusionment following the Exile, traditional Wisdom on this theme was found to be wanting. The verse dialogue in *Job* is at odds with the facile moralizing of the prose framework because the hero knows the facts do not support it (*Job* 12.6): "The tents of robbers are at peace." Qoheleth, too, knew that experience does not square with this inadequate theology (*Eccl* 2.18–23).

A SOLUTION TO THE PROBLEM AFTER DEATH WAS NOT KNOWN

Death was the great leveller for the composers of the Hebrew Bible: there was no settling of accounts on the other side of the grave. "The same fate comes to all, to the righteous and the wicked, to the good and the evil," muses Qoheleth (*Eccl* 9.1–6). Job has to admit that there is no solution in the direction of afterlife: unlike a tree which can sprout again, "mortals die, and are laid low" (*Job* 14.7–13).

UNTIL THE *WISDOM OF SOLOMON* REVEALS IMMORTALITY AND FINAL REWARD

The contribution of Greek philosophy to Jewish sapiential and historical tradition, evident in *Wisdom*, is an anthropology that enables theologians to envisage life for the soul after the death of the individual. Now a settling of accounts is possible, life with God for the just, a "hope full of immortality" (*Wis* 3.1–9), a complete retribution.

Further reading
C. Stuhlmueller, "Sickness and disease," *TBT* 27 (1989 No. 1), 5–9

D. E. Gowan, "Wealth and poverty in the Old Testament," *Int* 41 (1987 No. 4), 341–53

EXERCISES

1   What was your response to *Ecclesiastes*? Did you find yourself doubting the "inspiration" of this cheerless reflection? Check your expectations of inspired composition and the breadth of the range you will allow.

2. Phylis Trible includes *Judges* 19 in her *Texts of Terror*. Is "terror" the word you would use to describe your reaction to it? Do you think the author intended either response?

3. What sort of truth do you expect of the Bible? Is your expectation in line with the definition of biblical truth of Vatican II? How do fundamentalists' expectations of the truth of a text differ from yours?

4. *Job* and *Ecclesiastes* corrected or at least questioned a simplistic attitude to retribution. Do you think your attitude to evil and suffering (and ultimately God) is closer to theirs, or to earlier simplistic Wisdom, or to that of the New Testament?

CHAPTER 9

▼

A GRADUAL ENLIGHTENMENT

texts: *Job* 1–7; *Joshua* 9–11
biblical topic: Old Testament revelation
theological theme: the kingship of Yahweh

The divine influence that we believe operates in the composition of the Old Testament authors encourages us to find truth in their work. As Christians we also believe that truth is more conspicuous on the other side of the historical Incarnation and in the pages of the New Testament. Yet as human beings we have also to concede that the Word has been active in other communities, and that their traditions, biblical and otherwise, reflect the truth that comes from the one divine revealer—even if we are largely in ignorance of their traditions.

So we can hold that in our Bible we have the truth, nothing but the truth—but for the *whole* truth we may have to look elsewhere as well. To an even greater degree is this the case with the Old Testament. The divine inspiration of the authors ensures we have truth—"that truth which God wanted put into the sacred writings for the sake of our salvation" (*Dei Verbum* 11)—in all its pages, though we may have to exert ourselves to detect the saving truth of a particular passage. But the truth we find may shed only partial light on our problems. Job could take us further than his friends on the question of suffering and its explanation; but he was not able to penetrate a veil that lay over the complete answer at the time of composition.

We admit today that we do not have the complete answer to many of life's questions; we trust God's light will be shared still further with us, as we have benefited from it to a greater degree than our forebears. Within the Old Testament we can detect similar degrees of enlightenment on questions of life and history according as the divine revealer shared that light with various composers. Not all the traditions incorporated in its pages reflect the same clarity of knowledge of God—nor of God's designs for Israel and the world, as our readings will suggest.

109

Job 1–7

1) This book may have been called the supreme achievement of Hebrew Wisdom, arguably the greatest achievement of all biblical poetry, and one of the greatest works of world literature. But it has problems of its own, as our reading of these chapters alone reveals. The prose and verse sections seem to be conducting their own stories, not only unrelated but at variance: what is at issue in the prose—whether Job when afflicted will curse God—is not the issue of the verse. The proverbial "patience" of Job emerges only from the brief prose frame-work; the Job of the verse is anything but patient. Likewise the friends' role differs. The capricious God of the prose does not dominate the verse. The long verse chapters (whether prior or not) are interested in a basic sapiential question, the meaning of suffering; Eliphaz trots out the traditional equation of sin and suffering, which Job questions in the light of experience of the real world. And another theme enters, divine transcendence, which will assume greater importance as the book proceeds. Job challenges the transcendent God (and eventually has his day in court): "If I sin, what do I do to you, you watcher of humanity?" (7.20). The God of prose, friends and Job are different Gods, as necessarily are the attitudes to good and evil, suffering and prosperity.

2) Our perplexity has good grounds. The book is textually, linguistically and semantically difficult; the LXX version is considerably shorter than the Hebrew. Some chapters seem to be later additions, complicating the thought while perhaps intending to clarify it. The relation of prose and verse is unclear; critics speak of a "disjunction". Possibly the work is post-exilic. *Ezekiel* 14.14,20 knows a figure of legendary righteousness with the name Job, listed along with Noah and Danel. Despite the thorough (if not consistent) challenge the book offers to one aspect of traditional Wisdom and despite the poetry of many passages, one wonders why so many critics see it as a literary masterpiece.

3) In our re-reading we ignore the literary complexity and concentrate on the light that is being shed on the key question of the nature of God and reasons for human suffering. The prose settles for a capricious God, one who gives and takes away (1.21). Eliphaz depends on his fraternity's conviction (against the facts) of a predictable God who rewards and punishes in consistent response to good and evil. Job knows "the tents of robbers are at peace"—so what sort of God and providence/Wisdom can account for that? The book will conclude that divine Wisdom, perceptible in the universe, does not coincide with human wisdom (see Appendix 4, "Biblical Wisdom"). In the course of the book we have moved through a whole spectrum of human understanding of God and

his ways. If they did not penetrate that veil, they at least admitted there is one.

Further reading
N. Habel, *The Book of Job* (*OTL*), Philadelphia: Westminster, 1985
R. D. Moore, "The Integrity of Job," *CBQ* 45 (1983), 17–31
T. G. Long, "*Job*: second thoughts in the land of Uz," *Theology Today* 45 (1988 No. 1), 5–20

Joshua 9–11

1) Rather in the way we did in the case of *Judges* 19, we have conflicting emotions in response to this text. Joshua (a name perhaps meaning "Yahweh has saved": Greek *Jesus*) is obviously a very observant servant of the Lord and replica of Moses in this fidelity. He leads Israel against the Canaanite tribes and cities and kings with exemplary trust in the Lord, and the results are correspondingly positive. He knows how to honor a promise, so the Gibeonites escape with their lives (ch. 9). What we find hard to digest is that this obedience to divine commands meant destruction of everything and everybody belonging to the opposition: "He struck it with the edge of the sword, and every person in it." This "ban" is not an optional strategy of Joshua's: it is imposed by the Lord, and executed by the obedient general. "For it was the Lord's doings to harden (the Canaanites') hearts so that they would come against Israel in battle, in order that they might be utterly destroyed, and might receive no mercy, but be exterminated, just as the Lord had commanded Moses" (11.20). When we call to mind the God of *Jonah* who, unlike the reluctant prophet, is anxious that the Ninevites will be given the chance to repent, as in fact they do and are spared, the picture of this God and his prophet Joshua (as Ben Sira will call him: *Sir* 46.1) is at a far remove.

2) The book of *Joshua* has been seen variously as concluding the whole literary and theological movement of the Torah, thus called a "Hexateuch" (six books instead of five), and as the beginning with *Deuteronomy* of the Deuteronomist's work that stretches forward to *2 Kings*, leaving a shortened Torah or "Tetrateuch" of four books. The latter view allows us to see ancient traditions (including etiologies still visible in our chapters at 9.27; 10.27) subject to a theological review that highlights the efficacy of the Word of the Lord and the idealized figure of Joshua as a clone of Moses, foil to the disobedient Saul, and prototype of faithful kings David, Hezekiah and Josiah. This theological review at the hands of the Deuteronomist would have occurred in the

seventh century and again in a post-Deuteronomist form around the time of the Exile. No other country's literature in ancient times sought to interpret the significance of history in this way—just in annals or cyclic periods.

3) In re-reading the chapters we try to concentrate less on the events themselves than on discerning the evidence of the theological reviewers and their message, less on the quiet violence of the oft-recurring "there was none left who breathed" than on the ritualistic patterning of the material to bring out the refrain. The accent of the final author is on obedience and fulfilment of promise, we console ourselves with thinking, even if we would be grateful for the consolation of a prophet's God who would remind us, "Do not be afraid, I am with you" (*Is* 41.10). God and his purposes for *all* peoples are revealed in more appealing fashion in a *Jonah* and *Second Isaiah*, we feel.

Further reading
J. A. Soggin, *Joshua* (OTL)
M. H. Pope, "Devoted [the ban]," *IDB* I, 838–39
B. W. Anderson, "A holy war," *The Living World of the Old Testament*, 171–73

BIBLICAL TOPIC: OLD TESTAMENT REVELATION

The belief of the Jewish people is that their God makes himself known to them. At chosen moments and to special persons he reveals himself, as in the epiphany to Moses at Sinai and to prophets like Ezekiel, who nevertheless find no words adequate to describe the experience. Other prophets relay his words made known to them. He made himself known in their history, pre-eminently in their deliverance in the Exodus, accompanied by those great signs and wonders that they constantly recited in credal formulas. On their way through the wilderness to the land of promise he proceeded ahead as a pillar of cloud by day and a pillar of fire by night.

They could even recognize their Lord in the works of nature, and sing in the psalms (if in a minor key) of the Lord's creative works, the great lights, the sun to rule over the day, the moon and stars to rule over the night.

Divine self-communication

This revelation can best be understood as God's self-communication to the people so chosen. He shares with them life, truth and light about himself, themselves and all creation. The New Testament, recognizing Jesus as the supreme instance of this sharing, calls it *koinonia*, fellowship, participation, communion. The Vatican Council, from a Christian perspective, sees its biblical form this way (*Dei Verbum* 2):

> *In his goodness and wisdom God chose to reveal himself and to make known to us the hidden purpose of his will, by which through Christ, the Word made flesh, people have access to the Father in the Holy Spirit and come to share in the divine nature. Through this revelation, therefore, the invisible God out of the abundance of his love speaks to human beings as friends and lives among them, so that he may invite and take them into fellowship with him. This plan of revelation is realised by deeds and words having an inner unity: the deeds wrought by God in salvation history manifest and confirm the teaching and realities signified by the words, while the words proclaim the deeds and clarify the mystery contained in them.*

The Old Testament people had a privileged share in this revelation. For them prophets arose to interpret the events of salvation history, so that the people's historical writings could also be called "Prophets"; authors like the Yahwist and The Deuteronomist highlighted a pattern of events controlled by the Lord. Psalmists saw God's hand in nature, sages found evidence in life experience of divine retribution of good and evil.

A gradual revelation

It was a gradual revelation. Only gradually did the Old Testament people see the barbarity of practices like child sacrifice (the point of the Abraham and Isaac story in *Gn* 22) and complete destruction of enemies (as in *Jos* and *Ps* 137). The choice of the people of Israel, at first thought to be exclusive, is later seen to include other nations as well. The Wisdom literature begins with a facile equation of good with prosperity and evil with suffering, but events like the Exile led them to subject this to sceptical questioning. Gradually a sense of sin becomes more personal than merely communitarian, and individual responsibility comes to be highlighted. Death is final for most composers; only late in the Old Testament does the prospect of an afterlife emerge. The definitive incarnation of the Word had yet to occur.

Further reading

J. L. McKenzie, "Revelation," *NJBC* 1302–1304

J. Barr, "Revelation in history," *IDB Supp* 746–49

J. Blenkinsopp, "Yahweh and other deities," *Int* 40 (1986 No. 4), 354–66

C. Stuhlmueller, "History as the revelation of God in the Pentateuch," *Chicago Studies* 17 (1978 No. 1), 29–43

THEOLOGICAL THEME: THE KINGSHIP OF YAHWEH

(Be sure to read—aloud if possible—the passages nominated below.)

YAHWEH IS KING OF HEAVEN, EARTH AND ALL PEOPLES

Understandably in their cultural context the people of Israel envisaged their God as a monarch, but as one that surpassed all earthly kings. Their language of worship constantly addressed Yahweh as king of heavens, angels, hosts, all places (*Ps* 103.19–22). "Who would not fear you, O king of the nations?" asks Jeremiah (10.6–10).

YAHWEH AS KING CHOOSES ISRAEL AS HIS ROYAL PEOPLE

In relating to the people of Israel in covenant, Yahweh makes them his own possession and a royal people (*Exodus* 19.3–6). So the *Psalms* celebrate this choice of them over others: "The Lord, great king over all the earth, subdued peoples under us" (*Ps* 47).

YAHWEH EXERCISES A REIGN OF JUSTICE AND EQUITY

This king is to be praised, not simply for what he has done for the people, but as he is a lover of justice, having established equity, executed justice and righteousness (*Ps* 99). This king will judge the world with righteousness and the peoples with equity (*Ps* 98).

ISRAEL ACCEPTS YAHWEH AS KING

Both in response to being chosen and for the beneficent nature of his kingship, the people accept the rule of Yahweh. "The Lord is king!" is the theme of so many psalms of praise and thanksgiving. Their acceptance is unqualified.

YAHWEH IS ENTHRONED AS KING IN ZION

The people's liturgy celebrated Yahweh's enthronement in their midst, even if he reigns over the whole world. A number of psalms represent him taking up abode in the Temple in Jerusalem. *Psalm* 24 provides a ritual for those entering the Temple to celebrate the epiphany of Yahweh: "Lift up your heads, O gates! and be lifted up, O ancient doors! that the King of glory may come in."

ALTHOUGH HIS SWAY EXTENDS TO ALL CREATION

Though not a central concern of Old Testament thinkers, the whole cosmos is seen to fall under the sway of Yahweh. Second Isaiah assures the exiles of this in guaranteeing his action on their behalf in leading a new exodus (*Is* 43.14–21). Another enthronement hymn (*Ps* 97) depicts the mountains melting like wax before the Lord of all the earth.

YAHWEH BRINGS HIS PEOPLE DELIVERANCE AND SALVATION

Israel had ample occasion to sing the praises of their king whose reign meant deliverance from their enemies. The Song of Moses, or Miriam (*Exodus* 15), represents their Lord in colorful detail overthrowing Pharaoh's chariots and army, and concludes, "The Lord will reign forever and ever." The psalms frequently develop the same theme. *Lamentations* uses it to bemoan the absence of God's saving action on their behalf (5.19–22)

FROM THEM THE LORD EXPECTED OBEDIENCE

His reign would appear in their response to him. If, as *Psalm* 95 says, the Lord is a great God and a great King above all gods, the people are expected to worship, kneel and obey; but the wilderness provided examples of the contrary, hardness of heart and refusal to listen.

THEY REJECTED YAHWEH AS KING

Such refusal to heed his reign of justice and equity constituted rejection of Yahweh as king; the period of the Judges demonstrated such lawlessness

(*Jgs* 2.16–23). When later the people even wanted to ape the ways of foreigners by having an earthly king, the suggestion is treated—perhaps with northern prejudice—as a rejection of Yahweh himself (*1 Sam* 8.7–8).

EARTHLY KINGS RULED IN YAHWEH'S NAME

A more favorable interpretation of kingship in Israel is taken by both the Deuteronomist and the Chronicler, who see it sanctioned by Yahweh, even constituting an eternal dynasty (*2 Sam* 7.11–17; *1 Chronicles* 28.6–8). The delegated responsibility this entails is extended by the *Wisdom of Solomon* to all earthly kings (6.1–11).

A MESSIAH KING WILL BE THE IDEAL KING

The kings of Judah and Israel discharged their responsibility so imperfectly that prophets looked forward to another king to come in the future who would realize the failed ideals and be a prince of peace, bringing endless peace for the throne of David and his kingdom (*Is* 9.6–7).

THE LORD WILL REIGN OVER ALL NATIONS FROM JERUSALEM

That royal messianism envisages benefits not simply for one people but for many peoples and nations, who will come to the mountain of the Lord and the house of the God of Jacob; the Lord will reign over them in Mount Zion, and they shall beat their swords into ploughshares (*Mic* 4.1–7; *Is* 2.2–4).

Further reading
J. Gray, *The Biblical Doctrine of the Reign of God*, Edinburgh: Clark, 1979

A. Weiser, *The Psalms* (*OTL*), 5th ed, ET, London: SCM, 1962

G. T. Sheppard, "Theology and the book of *Psalms*," *Int* 46 (1992 No. 2), 143–55

EXERCISES

1. Can you see, as our text says of *Job*, that "the God of prose [prologue & epilogue], friends and Job are different Gods"? Specify the differences in relation to the problem of good and evil, suffering and prosperity.

2. The "ban" we find in *Joshua* strikes us as a frightful institution, especially coming from the Lord's own direction. Can you appreciate how it arises out of a particular period of Israel's history and theology?

3. In what you have read of the Old Testament so far, can you detect a developing revelation? Be specific. Does this also suggest something of the relationship of Old and New Testaments?

4. Read through a number of the *Psalms*, such as those cited in the theological theme but also others, and see how frequent is reference to the kingship of Yahweh. Why is it such a recurring theme?

CHAPTER 10

MAKING SENSE OF THE WORD

texts: *Jonah; Hosea* 1–3
biblical topic: interpretation
theological theme: people, community

The New Testament will say of the Word that he came to his own but his own did not accept him. The Old Testament, too, registers this reluctance to accept the Word in the sense spoken. Jeremiah performs his prophetic function of relaying the Word of the Lord—a distasteful Word, admittedly—to King Jehoiakim and his court in Jerusalem, only to have the king show his contempt for it by burning the scroll on which it was recorded (*Jer* 36). Isaiah of Jerusalem presents the Lord condemning his people for forbidding the seers to see and for directing the prophets thus, "Do not prophesy to us what is right; speak to us smooth things, prophesy illusions" (*Is* 30.10). The Lord's retort is drastic: because you reject this Word, you will be smashed like a potter's vessel.

There has always been a problem about acceptance of the Word in the sense spoken, as there is in accepting Jesus as Word enfleshed. There can be outright rejection, there can be deliberate distortion, there can be the misinterpretation of ignorance. The former two imply malice, and require repentance. To rectify the latter, good will and enlightenment are required if obstacles on our part are to be removed. Hermeneutical skills can be developed in readers and listeners to the scriptural Word in the Old Testament; it calls for these skills as the New Testament admitted of both Jewish and Pauline Scriptures. "There are some things in them hard to understand, which the ignorant and unstable twist to their own destruction, as they do the other scriptures" (*2 Pet* 3.16).

Interpretation–"hermeneutics" in biblical parlance–is about finding meaning, the right meaning. Every word, human and divine, is subject to this search: Jesus has been subject to it, Shakespeare has been, the Old Testament Word must surely be. *Jonah* and *Hosea*, interpreted variously over the years, illustrate the challenge involved.

121

Jonah

1) This is a really enjoyable story to read, and one that can hardly be taken at face value. The idea of a prophet being instructed by the Lord to go to that hell on earth, Nineveh, and instead heading off in the opposite direction, being deposited back at point A after adventures on ship and in the fish's belly, eventually going to the Assyrians' city and converting them all with but a few words, grieving over this rapid conversion and being upbraided by the Lord for his dog-in-the-manger attitude–it's all a bit much to take as straight history. We can see the bold prophetic message: God's mercy is available to everyone, irrespective of race or record. Israel's prophets also come in for satire, Jonah being more concerned for his protective bush than the fate of a whole city. He is pious enough (the psalm in chapter 2 a little too obtrusively so?), knowing that the Lord is "a gracious God and merciful, slow to anger, and abounding in steadfast love" (4.2), though his God is not the God of the patriarchs but "the Lord, the God of heaven, who made the sea and dry land" (1.9). This sapiential accent on creation is evident also in the concern for the welfare of Nineveh's animals. In fact, there are several indications of a Wisdom perspective to the book, particularly its universalism (see Appendix 4, "Biblical Wisdom"). There is clearly a message to this (surely quite late) fantasy.

2) Scholars can tell us little of the book's author, we find. The reference to the eighth century figure of the same name mentioned at *2 Kgs* 14.25 is surely literary artifice, the book's language (with many Aramaisms) and message suggesting a much later date. The Assyrians are now less of a real than a legendary threat to be treated so lightly, so a lot of time must have elapsed since the eighth century. Opinion is divided on the original placement of the psalm in chapter 2, some seeing it as a later addition.

3) Interpreting the book as prophetic fiction with a didactic purpose, in re-reading it we appreciate the gentle irony with which the author treats current attitudes to Israel's exclusive claims on Yahweh's love and mercy and prophetic practices arising from this parochial view. The point is well made with great economy (the psalm excepted) by narrative of a wicked city responding to a few words of warning rather than by mere preaching of this radical doctrine. There is much more narrative, much less oracular statement, than is usual in prophetic material. It is a fun book, but very serious - provided it is taken in the right sense. It is thus a challenge to fundamentalists.

Further reading
J. Mulrooney, "The spiritual pilgrimage of Jonah," *TBT* 29 (1991 No. 3), 163–66
J. F. McCann, "Jonah: Doctor Strangelove," *TBT* 27 (1989 No. 5), 298–303

Hosea 1–3

1) Another case of a prophet getting a raw deal, like Jonah—if we are to take the text at face value. But there is no fun here. We are well rooted in a threatening historical situation, with those references to the situation of Judah and especially Israel in the late eighth century with Assyria on the horizon (see the timeline, p. 6, and p. 7). Samaria has yet to fall, but Hosea is saying the writing is on the wall for the northern kingdom. Through the story of a strange, obviously ill-fated marriage and the birth of children with prophetic names, the recipients of the prophecy would get a clear message of the political and religious infidelity of the northern kingdom and the threat of covenant breakdown. The talk of Baals ("proprietors", local gods) and the marriage imagery suggest reversion to Canaanite fertility rites, abhorrent to covenant morality, fidelity, covenant love ("kindness," which is an insipid translation in some versions). Altogether a messy scene; we know its disastrous sequel. We ask ourselves whether the prophet's life story is to be taken literally or figuratively, and whether the marriage in chapter 3 is to be seen as a remarriage after divorce or a restatement of the original marriage.

2) We know nothing else about Hosea son of Beeri. The kings mentioned at the outset help date the historical reference and political situation (see list of kings below). Strangely, most of these kings are from Judah; do we have a southern editor of this northern prophet? Gomer's name is not allegorical, so perhaps the marriage is real. Baalism and its practices of cultic prostitution were rampant in the north before its fall. As often in the prophetic books, the assembling of oracles into a final text can be haphazard, so we may have a lack of sequence in these chapters, but the drift is clear. It is the interpretation that is difficult, whether to take the narrative at face value.

The Kings of Judah and Israel

| David | c. 1010–970 |
| Solomon | c. 970–931 |

Judah		Israel	
Rehoboam	931–913	Jeroboam I	931–910
Abijah	913–911		
		Nadab	910–909
Asa	911–870	Baasha	909–886
		Elah	886–885
		Zimri	885
		Omri	885–874
Jehoshaphat	870–848	Ahab	874–853
		Ahaziah	853–852
Jehoram	848–841	Jeroham	853–841
Ahaziah	841		
Athaliah	841–835	Jehu	841–814
Joash	835–796		
		Jehoahaz	814–789
Amaziah	796–781	Jehoash	798–783
Uzziah	781–740	Jeroboam II	783–743
		Zechariah	743
		Shallum	743
Jotham	740–736	Menahem	743–738
		Pekahiah	738–737
Ahaz	736–716	Pekah	737–732
		Hoshea	732–724
		Fall of Samaria 721	
Hezekiah	716–687		
Manasseh	687–642		
Amon	642–640		
Josiah	640–609		
Jehoahaz	609		
Jehoiakim	609–597		
Jehoiachin	697		
Zedekiah	597–587		
Fall of Jerusalem 587			

3) Ignoring textual problems, we re-read the text and ponder its prophetic message of fidelity to the covenant "as at the time when she came out of the land of Egypt" (2.15). The message from the marriage story is clear: cease infidelity if you wish to be my people and to share my covenant love, my "pity". The wife's (and people's) infidelity is spelled out in graphic detail (2.4–17), as is the hope of reconciliation (2.18–25). We will never know whether to interpret the marriage story as historical fact, but the religious truth is stark and unmistakable.

Further reading
S. Terrien, *The Elusive Presence*, 241–45
M. Paolantonio, "God as husband," *TBT* 27 (1989 No. 5), 299–303

BIBLICAL TOPIC: INTERPRETATION

Obviously, there are various ways to interpret language, spoken and written, and to interpret literary works. Jesus and his contemporaries clearly took the book of *Jonah* as straight fact (cf. *Mt* 12.40), whereas we see its prophetic purpose differently. A principal concern of ours is to determine the intention of the speaker/writer and to align our understanding with that—though once the speaker/writer is detached from the utterance, we have less clear guidance in our search. Shakespeare is no longer available for guidance on the interpretation of *Henry VIII*; we notice in our reading that the author's sympathies seem to be with Catherine in the first half of the play, and with Anne in the second—but the text has a life of its own now and is open to the interpretation of individual readers (who may not be aware of damage to the original text in a fire at *The Globe* and rewriting by another dramatist).

Recognizing the genre

So we endeavor to reach the intention of the composer through his (now written) works. We noted in previous chapters the need to recognize the precise kind of composition chosen by the composer to express his intention; and we have just seen how proper interpretation of *Hosea* depends on determining whether or not the author is employing historical narrative or allegory in describing the marriage. Vatican II in its statement on biblical interpretation, or hermeneutics (to use the common Greek term), stressed this further obvious point:

> *For the correct understanding of what the sacred author wanted to assert, due attention must be paid to the customary and characteristic styles of*

perceiving, speaking and narrating which prevailed at the time of the sacred writer, and to the customs people normally followed at that period in their everyday dealings with one another (Dei Verbum 12).

If, for instance, the Torah incorporates a presentation of God's relationship with the people in the form of a political alliance in vogue at the time, we should learn what we can of that treaty form so as to determine, for example, how we should interpret the Ten Commandments within that context. If we acknowledge the attitudes of authors accustomed to bracketing out of consideration a woman's viewpoint, we should be sensitive to this in reading texts like *Judges* 19 and much antifeminist Wisdom material.

A fuller sense

While the community for whom Old Testament material was composed would interpret it in one way, other communities later—of Judaism or Christianity—might view it differently. Those who theologized and wrote about Jesus would see in Old Testament texts a fuller (i.e. more than literal) sense in certain key passages. Second Isaiah's songs about a mysterious servant of the Lord suffering for a guilty people appealed to the evangelists as referring to the Jesus of the Passion stories, as did the psalms of the Royal Sufferer (like *Ps* 22)—a fuller sense than the original author was aware of. Christian liturgy and preaching would follow in this line of usage.

Typology

A wider challenge for Christian readers of the Old Testament is to find its meaning as a totality: has it any relevance to Christians today? The early Church, particularly in the Alexandrian school of interpretation (by contrast with the school of Antioch, more attached to the literal sense of Scripture), followed a method of typology. By this approach certain figures and events could be recognized as foreshadowing later realities in the life of Jesus: the sacrifice of Isaac, the Passover, the figure of David were thus seen as types of the person and life of Jesus, the antitype. One limitation to this hermeneutical method is that it deals only with a fraction of the Old Testament and leaves so much irrelevant.

The mystery of Christ

A more comprehensive approach was adopted by those, like Paul, who looked for a total pattern of God's dealings with the people and all creation revealed in the Old Testament and continuing beyond it. Paul spoke of this as the mystery of Christ—"mystery" in the sense of a divine design/plan/purpose for all things which stretches "from before the foundation of the world," gathers in the story of the Old Testament people, and reaches a focal point in the Paschal Mystery of Jesus. (A task remains to gather also the religious history of other people into the mystery of Christ.)

Levels of meaning

So there can be various levels of meaning in any Old Testament text. We strive to discover the meaning intended by the composer, using all the clues available. A further level of meaning depends on the placement of the text within the whole canon. The songs of the Suffering Servant occur now within the work of Second Isaiah—itself combined with other prophetic works in the book of *Isaiah*—and stand in our Christian Bible alongside Gospel texts that deliberately evoke those songs in relation to Jesus. They thus acquire great depth of meaning of which the original author was unaware. In addition to this canonical sense there is the meaning the text has for me now in my reading of it, affected as I am by my situation (as the composer was by his). Hopefully we can allow our reading of Old Testament texts to bring this richness of meaning to our consciousness. (We look at interpretation in greater depth in ch. 14, "Further critical approaches".)

Further reading
R. E. Brown, S. M. Schneiders, "Hermeneutics," *NJBC* 1146–65
I. Nowell, "Typology: a method of interpretation," *TBT* 28 (1990 No. 2), 70–76
C. Osiek, "Literal meaning and allegory," *TBT* 29 (1991 No. 5), 261–66

THEOLOGICAL THEME: PEOPLE, COMMUNITY

(Be sure to read—aloud if possible—the texts nominated below.)

A SMALL, MIXED GROUP OF TRIBES BECAME A PEOPLE

There was nothing attractive or united about the mixed group that came out of Egypt under the leadership of Moses. The Torah refers to "a crowd of mixed ancestry" (*Exodus* 12.38; *Numbers* 11.4) that began the march.

Deuteronomy reminds the covenanted people later that they were "the fewest of all peoples" (*Dt* 7.7) at the time, with nothing about them to win the favor of the Lord.

YET THE LORD CHOSE THIS PEOPLE, THIS SPECIAL POSSESSION

Remarkable, then, was the initiative of Yahweh to choose them to become "my treasured possession out of all the peoples" (*Ex* 19.5)—such was their conviction in retrospect. The prophets console or upbraid the people on the same basis of choice, whether at Sinai or in the patriarchs: "You, Israel, my servant, Jacob, whom I have chosen, the offspring of Abraham, my friend" (*Is* 41.8–9).

TO THE EXCLUSION OF OTHER PEOPLES

At least as the Old Testament often interprets it, this choice was exclusive, disregarding other peoples. "The Lord your God has chosen you out of all the peoples on earth to be his people, his treasured possession," Moses in *Deuteronomy* reminds them before insisting on their lack of title to this (7.6). The book of *Jonah* we saw having to militate against this deep-seated conviction late in Old Testament times.

WHO WERE DESERVING OF HOSTILITY

Not surprisingly for a small people surrounded by stronger, often ill-dis-posed nations, Israel's literature abounds in oracles against these countries. The oracles are usually presented as "the word of the Lord concerning Israel" forecasting a dreadful fate for them: "This shall be the plague with which the Lord will strike all the peoples that wage war against Jerusalem: their flesh shall rot while they are still on their feet" (*Zechariah* 14.12).

AND YET THROUGH ISRAEL WOULD RECEIVE BLESSING

Calmer spirits could see, on the other hand, that Israel had a role in the world of the Near East to bring peace and blessing, at least in the long term. The very opening of the people's story in the Yahwist's patriarchal narrative envisages blessings coming through Abraham to Israel and through it to "all the families of the earth" (*Gn* 12.1–3). This sharing of blessings is a feature of messianic prophecies (*Micah* 4.1–4).

THE LORD RELATED TO ISRAEL IN COVENANT

The exclusive relationship of the Lord to Israel is expressed in political terms as covenant, treaty, alliance - a predictable presentation in the world of the time conscious of the kind of support small nations stood to gain from the day's superpowers. So the Torah speaks in these terms, and prophets like *Hosea* we saw restating it if also allowing for an element of love between the partners.

AS A COMMUNITY THEY WERE TO BE FAITHFUL

It followed that the whole community of Israel was beholden to the Lord for this remarkable initiative, which meant special care and protection for every member; and they would all respond with national fidelity. *Deuteronomy* has Moses spell out for the people, directly after the Decalogue, that "you and your children and your children's children may fear the Lord your God all the days of your life, and keep all his decrees and his commandments that I am commanding you, so that your days may be long" (*Dt* 6.2).

AS A COMMUNITY THEIR INFIDELITIES WERE PUNISHABLE

Covenant required community fidelity; breach of it had community implications. Even though *Hosea* speaks of the intimacy of the relationship, he sees its breakdown as affecting everyone alike, who have thus become "not pitied" and "not my people" (*Hos* 1). The Deuteronomist is at pains to highlight community solidarity in sin and in punishment: after detailing the failings of Israel's kings, he concludes, "The Lord rejected all the descendants of Israel; he punished them" (*2 Kings* 17.20).

THE PEOPLE BECAME A NATION UNDER DAVID

The motley group of tribes and clans to whom Yahweh manifested himself in the wilderness and who took possession of Canaan finally attained nationhood under David, who secured their community loyalty and gave them a national center in Jerusalem after dislodging the Jebusites from the stronghold of Zion (*I Chronicles* 11.1–10).

BUT BECAME DIVIDED, CONQUERED, EXILED

It was not long, however, before this newly united nation fell apart after David and Solomon (*1 Kings* 12.16–20). The story of the two kingdoms is also one of community infidelity, if we can believe The Deuteronomist, who diagnoses the cause of eventual conquest by foreign invaders (*2 Kings* 17). Even The Chronicler paints a depressing picture of the community of Judah returned from Exile: "Here we are, slaves to this day, slaves in the land which you gave to our ancestors to enjoy" (*Nehemiah* 9.36).

YET CONTINUED AS A PEOPLE TO HAVE MESSIANIC EXPECTATIONS

Prophetic and apocalyptic literature continued to look forward to a time when the nation would return to its original power and status, under an ideal ruler; "a remnant of Jacob, surrounded by many peoples, shall be like the dew from the Lord, . . . like a lion among the animals of the forest" (*Micah* 5.7–9). Even north and south would be reunited (5.3). For Haggai the rebuilding of the Temple is harbinger of this revival (*Haggai* 2.6–9).

Further reading
S. D. McBride, "Polity of the covenant people: the book of *Deuteronomy*," *Int* 41 (1987 No. 3), 229–44
J. L. McKenzie, "Israel—God's covenanted people," *NJBC* 1295–1301

EXERCISES

1. Do you think you grasp the author's ironical and didactic purpose in the book of *Jonah*? What would be lost if a fundamentalist wanted to take it as an historical account?

2. How do you see the story of Hosea's marriage: fact or allegory? Does the prophetic message differ if one interprets it one way or the other?

3. Can you think of other parts of the Bible where you have grown up with an inadequate, even fundamentalist, understanding of the nature of the material and the sense intended?

4. Does the marriage imagery employed in *Hosea* and elsewhere in the Old Testament for the relationship between Yahweh and the people lend to it a depth missing from more legalistic ways of thinking of Church, spirituality, religion?

CHAPTER 11

▼

GETTING THE SENSE WRONG

texts: *Daniel* 7–12; *Zechariah* 12–14
biblical topic: fundamentalism
theological theme: fidelity, faith

Medieval religious art is evidence of the fact that we all like to make God in our own image. Figures and landscapes are depicted in the style familiar to the artists, even down to details of medieval garments and buildings, let alone the cast of features of a Madonna and child—Florentine or Siennese rather than Palestinian. If the Word is to become incarnate, it will be on our terms and in our preferred style. Anything else can lead us out of our own world, our own culture, where we feel less secure. It also calls for greater exertion on our part to understand forms of expression we may not be familiar with.

This kind of reductionism can very much impede our meeting the Word incarnate in the texts of the Old Testament, where variety and diversity of expression are of the essence. The Word is very much inculturated there, and the culture is not ours. We may be accustomed to law and statute, prayer and proverb; biblical history and prophecy are, however, not our normal diet, and apocalyptic visions and landscapes are as foreign to us as we now find the medieval nativities. To recognize the diversity of these forms of expression is one thing; to get to know their different features and purposes takes much more effort. Incarnation brings a richness that is also a challenge: what a pity if readers forfeit the prodigality of the Word by preferring to read all texts alike, as it would be a pity to reduce *Matthew, Mark, Luke* and *John* to one standard-issue portrait of Jesus.

To some readers of Old Testament (and other culturally conditioned) texts, the task is simply to crack a nut: within every shell, of whatever color and texture, there lies a nut, and the sooner we discard the shell we can get to the nut, the kernel. To them, all nuts are basically similar, and the shells of no account. So all Old Testament texts convey a similar truth, historical truth, no matter which outward form of expression is called into the service of truth. Those who come to your door peddling biblical

135

texts—usually apocalyptic texts like *Daniel* or *Revelation*—want you to accept them as truth, usually historical truth, and change your life accordingly. The different nuances of Yahwist and Elohist in the Torah, the distinction in theological outlook between a Deuteronomist and a Chronicler in rehearsing Israel's history, the subtle reworking by Ben Sira of the well-worn creation story to bring out a universalist Wisdom approach (*Sir* 16.26–17.17)—all these are not the "truth" the fundamentalist has determined the Word must convey, and like a shell they are jettisoned. God is made in his or her own image—and generally is not pretty.

Daniel 7–12

1) This is really technicolor material, the stuff of "biblical" movies: vision after vision, great beasts coming up out of the sea, heavenly courts, old men on fiery thrones, battles between rams and goats, kings from various periods, angels giving heavenly oracles, prophecies of everlasting life, numbers without end, the sealing of the book. It is as hard to take this at face value as it is to follow either the chronological references or the meaning of the symbolic narratives. Anyone wishing to read historical significance into it, for present or future, would have a field day. The action in this half of the book seems to be set in the Babylonian and Persian periods, to judge from mention of "Belshazzar of Babylon," Darius and Cyrus; the four visions thus stretch over a lengthy span. The employment of dreams and visions, angels conveying interpretations, the great sweep of history "until the time of the end"—all suggest this is apocalyptic material, and thus arising out of a period of oppression and persecution of the Jewish people, perhaps by the Seleucids in the second century that gave rise also to the *Maccabees*. So the Daniel is unlikely to be the character of that name in *Ezekiel* or other biblical books.

2) Reference to the scholars confirms our suggestion of composition late in Old Testament times and precisely in the period of the proverbially evil Seleucid general Antiochus IV Epiphanes (whom we met above in chapter 4). The language of the book is a mixture of Hebrew (all but chapter 7 of this half) and Aramaic, also suggesting late composition. Yet the author, or authors, of the various visions is projecting the narrative back several centuries to the times of earlier empires in which Jews suffered. We have to guess who is meant by "King Belshazzar" and "Darius the Mede," since neither is accurate historically. The vision in chapter 7 of the four empires—presumably Babylonian, Median, Persian and Greek—and the last horn of the fourth beast, referring apparently to Antiochus, is significant from a New Testament viewpoint

for its picture of the Son of Man on which the evangelists call for their presentation of Jesus. The Greek versions of the book contain three extra stories, now in chapters 13–14.

3) Piecing together all the occult clues, fascinating though it may be to certain devotees of trivial pursuits, is to miss the author's purpose: the encouragement of Jews in the face of pressure to abandon Jewish ways and adopt hellenistic practices. The toppling of enemies; the insistence that no matter what discrepancies have occurred with the biblical timeline for salvation (in *Dn* 9), the Lord of history and the Lord's angelic agents are still in command; the sweep of history that reaches to everlasting life for some (ch. 12: a unique biblical insight)—all this is meant to restore confidence, even if much license is taken along the way and the facts get fudged. To find in it historical precision or accurate prediction would be to mistake the dress in which the Word comes to us in this text. We await with dread the moviemaker's rendition, which will only reinforce this misinterpretation, like all such movies.

Further reading

C. L. Kuhn, "The fine line: the relevance of apocalyptic today," *TBT* 28 (1990 No. 5), 267–69

B. W. Anderson, "The Apocalypse of *Daniel*," *The Living World of the Old Testament*, 576–91

N. Porteous, *Daniel (OTL)*

Zechariah 12–14

1) Once more we despair of finding an obvious historical path amongst these oracular statements. There is talk of Judah, Jerusalem, the house of David, Egypt, and all are promised various fates, as though these are still in the future—which would mean an early date of composition. But there is also plenty of mention of "that day," a day that is coming, the day of the Lord: a stock apocalyptic phrase, suggesting past events are in fact being used to forecast some vague future. The New Testament found material for the presentation of the suffering Jesus in "the one whom they have pierced" (12.10) and the mysterious martyred shepherd of chapter 13; one is reminded of Second Isaiah's suffering servant. There is good news and bad news: Jerusalem is in for a cleansing from sin and impurity, as is the Temple; prophets do not deserve to continue; priests get no mention at all. But the Lord will become king over all the earth, and foreign nations will not prevail. Who precisely is meant as beneficiary of these apocalyptic oracles is far from clear.

2) Scholars have not done much better than we have in our reading. The book of *Zechariah* seems divisible into at least two parts, after chapter 8 and perhaps again after chapter 11, allowing for perhaps three authors. The prophet "Zechariah son of Berechiah son of Iddo" (1.1), responsible for chapters 1–8, quite likely exercised a ministry among the restored community in Jerusalem in the late sixth century; but authorship of "Deutero-Zechariah" is less clear, perhaps attributable to the Hellenistic period. It is agreed that our chapters are "less directly and concretely interested in contemporary historical reality than were those of earlier prophets, and that they show more concern with a future lacking historical specificity and portrayed in colors which have a tone that becomes more mythological as the apocalyptic tendency is more fully developed" (*NJBC* 353).

3) In re-reading these chapters of Deutero-Zechariah we are reminded of a style of preaching in our own community that has generally receded today—plenty of colorful, threatening, dire warnings, in the mode of "See, a day is coming for the Lord" (14.1). To be sure, Jerusalem or Rome or Canterbury can always do with the institutional purification demanded here. It would, however, be prostituting the Word to claim contemporary relevance for historical references in these texts other than what the New Testament was intending in evoking these chapters as *testimonia* of the suffering Jesus in Gospel Passion stories. Apocalyptic has its value, once we recognize it as such and not as historical narrative. Does our own time and culture generate true apocalyptic (as distinct from the mindless violence of "Apocalypse Now"), or do we too require a time of persecution to produce it?

Further reading

P. D. Hanson, "Book of *Zechariah*," IDB Supp 982–83

——, "Apocalyptic literature," *The Hebrew Bible and its Modern Interpreters*, 465–488

G. W. McRae, "Eschatology," *Chicago Studies* 17 (1978 No. 1), 59–66

BIBLICAL TOPIC: FUNDAMENTALISM

Our task in reading the Old Testament (and New), as we have insisted from the outset, is to achieve a meeting with the Word incarnate in the text. That term "incarnate" is as much a challenge as is the Word in person: to recognize in all the cultural features of any particular passage of any particular place and period the Word enfleshed there. Not, as we noted, in the sense of cracking a nut to discard the shell; we do not need McLuhan to tell us the medium is part and parcel of the message, as we do not need the history of theology to remind us of the dangerous docetism that would pry divinity from humanity in Jesus and still claim to respect the divine economy. We recognize the Old Testament Word incarnate in prophecy as in proverb, in psalm as in apocalyptic. So our "biblical topics" in previous chapters have covered matters such as authorship and composition, biblical criticism, culture, historical composition, literary genres, biblical truth, interpretation—all topics intended to discourage our ignoring the particular form in which the Word comes to us in Old Testament texts.

Truth and truth

It is a fundamentalist who would prefer to ignore the features of enculturation of the Word in biblical texts, or would simply seek to peel them away like a shell or skin to find truth within. The fundamentalist would not subscribe to the principle enunciated by Vatican II that "truth is proposed and expressed in a variety of ways, depending on whether a text is history of one kind or another, or whether its form is that of prophecy, poetry, or some other type of speech." For a fundamentalist, *Jonah* and *Daniel* tell a story; all stories are historical; therefore, Jonah's visit to Nineveh and Daniel's dealings with "King Belshazzar" are to be taken at face value. A fundamentalist, of course, has greater difficulties with the discrepancies between different biblical creation stories, flood narratives, decalogues, genealogies (of Cain, for example), local and tribal names in the various strands of the Torah—preferring not to admit development and change in the course of literary composition.

Education in change

Biblical fundamentalism is but one manifestation of a wider tendency to distrust and avoid evidence of change and development. Church life and teaching, politics, economics, and social behavior can come under the same anxiety to retain continuity and eliminate questioning "criticism" in its positive sense. Admittedly, people have not always been given good grounding in the basis for change—in Church teaching, in biblical education, in liturgical practice. That is a fault of educators, like biblical scholars, some of whom have ignored the principle of Pope Pius XII that "the sacred books were not given by God to satisfy people's curiosity or to provide them with an object of study and research" (*Divino Afflante Spiritu* 51). An antidote to fundamentalism lies in better education so that people will not have an unreasonable fear of scholarship and critical approaches (through a book like this, for instance). Laziness and anti-intellectualism, however, may be proof against these measures.

Need of study

Incarnation implies hard work: we must make an effort to take account of the enculturation of the Word, whether in the Old Testament or in Jesus. A charismatic approach that suggests that one need only wait for inspiration to strike is an arrogance that ignores the sacramentalism of God's dealings—in Scripture as in other ways.

Further reading
M. C. Boys, "Educational and pastoral approaches to Scripture: Fundamentalism," *PACE* 11 (1981)

E. LaVerdiere, "Fundamentalism," *TBT* 21 (1983 January), 5–11

R. P. McBrien, "Teaching Catholicism today: The challenge of fundamentalism," *PACE* 16 (1986)

R. C. Hill, *Breaking the Bread of the Word. Principles of Teaching Scripture* (see "fundamentalism" in General Index)

THEOLOGICAL THEME: FIDELITY, FAITH

(Be sure to read—aloud if possible—the passages nominated below.)

ISRAEL'S FAITH RESTED ON THE LORD'S TRUSTWORTHINESS

Of all the psalms *Psalm* 117 reduces Israel's beliefs in all Yahweh's attributes to two: covenant love and the Lord's trustworthiness, faithfulness, fidelity, *'emeth*. That underpins the community's faith. In another classic statement of this truth, from the prophet Habbakuk in the late seventh century (which the New Testament will take and twist somewhat), Yahweh assures the people that their fidelity depends on his (*Hab* 2.2–5).

YAHWEH IS ABOVE ALL TRUSTWORTHY AND LOVING

So Israel counts on and confesses the Lord's love and faithfulness. It is an accent that comes through alongside that on punitive jealousy: compare the Yahwist's version of the remaking of the covenant (*Ex* 34.6–7), where the Lord is "a God abounding in steadfast love and faithfulness," with the Elohist's version of the initial ceremony (*Ex* 20.5–6). The psalmists love to couple the two, faithfulness and love (e.g. *Ps* 57.3,10).

AND IS ALONE THE BASIS OF PEACE AND CONTENTMENT

So Yahweh is a fortress and a rock, a secure refuge, a strong city, and thus deserving of faith and trust if peace is to be won. So say the psalmists, and the prophets like Isaiah (*Is* 26.2–4). No trust can be placed in false prophets, says Jeremiah, who see the basis for peace elsewhere (*Jer* 14.13–16).

THE COVENANT, A RELATIONSHIP BETWEEN FIDELITY AND FAITH

The special relationship between Yahweh and the people rested on this dual initiative: the Lord's supremely trustworthy favor towards them and their response in faith. Jeremiah has the Lord invoking his own truth and justice as the basis for repentance (*Jer* 4.1–2).

THE LAW GAINED ITS VALIDITY AND CLAIM FROM YAHWEH'S FIDELITY

The biblical composers—of Torah, prophecy and psalms—are concerned to root the Law in its many stipulations in something beyond mere divine arbitrariness: Yahweh's fidelity, truth, trustworthiness, *'emeth*. So says the psalmist in that long meditation on the Law, *Psalm* 119 (e.g. v. 160).

THE PEOPLE RESPONDED IN FAITH TO YAHWEH'S TRUSTWORTHINESS

The proper response to divine fidelity is faith: in believing the believer could count on God remaining faithful. So said Habakkuk in the seventh century, so said Third Isaiah in the sixth in speaking of "the God of faithfulness" (*Is* 65.16).

FAITH IS SAYING "AMEN" TO GOD

For Old Testament theologians faith is acceptance of and response to the God of faithfulness, *'emeth*. That attitude found expression in a word from the same root, *Amen*. In *Deuteronomy* the covenant is sealed with a series of "Amens" to the curses uttered by the Levites against covenant breaches (*Dt* 27.11–26).

A LIFE OF FAITH IS ONE THAT REFLECTS YAHWEH'S LOVE AND FIDELITY

Faith implies observance of the Law. The prophets saw inobservance as stemming from lack of faith. "There is no faithfulness or loyalty," says Hosea in lamenting swearing, lying and murder, stealing, adultery and bloodshed (*Hos* 4.1–3). The crisis Jeremiah encounters comes from the fact that there is no one who acts justly and seeks truth (*Jer* 5.1–3).

FAILURE TO HAVE THIS FAITH HAS SERIOUS CONSEQUENCES

Whereas the due response of faith to God's initiative brings life, failure to respond is punishable—as *Deuteronomy* reminds the signatories of the covenant (*Dt* 28.64–67). Isaiah reminds his listeners that the rock that is the God of faithfulness can also crush the mighty in favor of the poor and needy (*Is* 26.4–6).

THE FULL MEANING OF FAITH IS FOUND IN CLOSE RELATIONSHIP WITH YAHWEH

A life of faith is much more than mere observance of law, important though such fidelity is. It earns the reward of the intimate relationship of which Hosea speaks, being taken by Yahweh "for my wife in righteousness and in justice, in steadfast love and in mercy, . . . taken for my wife in faithfulness" (*Hos* 2.19–20).

Further reading
B. W. Anderson, "Abraham, the friend of God," *Int* 42 (1988 No. 4), 353–66

J. A. Sullivan, "The 'existential' faith of the Hebrews," *TBT* 27 (1989 No. 5), 288–92

J. M. Ward, "Faith, faithfulness in the Old Testament," *IDB Supp* 329–32

EXERCISES

1 Do you feel at home with the apocalyptic material in *Daniel*—dreams and visions, angels and beasts, vast extent of time, puzzling symbols? Is the author's general drift clear, if not each symbolic detail?

2. Can you recall preaching of the kind employed by Deutero-Zechariah, with an accent on divine retribution in a Day of the Lord, threats and warnings? Are we meant to take this, whether preaching or biblical composition, at face value? How should we take it?

3. Education in the Scriptures is the key to arresting the progress of fundamentalism. Bible movies have the opposite effect, treating as realistic what people should be led to see as some other form of expression. Examine one such movie that fails in this way.

4. Faith is sometimes misrepresented as a funny inside feeling, about which one can do nothing. The Old Testament would have none of that, and sees the way to develop faith. Suggest how such a biblical understanding of faith can help remove that misrepresentation.

CHAPTER 12

▼

SEEKING THE LORD

texts: *Psalms* 8, 22, 23, 119, 136; *Ezekiel* 18
biblical topic: Old Testament spirituality
theological theme: hope, afterlife

The Old Testament is not a history book, secular or religious, but basically a theological story. We see in it a long series of theologians reflecting on "the God who acts" in favor of a people. Many of these theologians have as well a personal story of a search after God, like Hosea and Jeremiah. They also tell of figures engaged in the same search and gifted with remarkable spiritual experiences, like Elijah and Job. The search and experience of women, even such as Deborah, is less at the focus of attention.

To an extent we can identify with the people of the Old Testament in our own search, or at least admire or learn from them.

So the Old Testament, and the Bible generally, has proved a fertile source for readers' spiritual development. This is as it should be: theology is not just a cognitive experience but a faith-filled and faith-nourishing endeavor. As one of the great medieval commentators remarked, "After theology, only the beatific vision." Readers (and listeners) through the ages have found in these scriptures insight into God's ways, guidance in the good life, consolation in times of tribulation. Jesus, who knew these scriptures well, even unconsciously resorted to them for expression of anguished appeal to the Father in his darkest moment. And the evangelists love to fill out his significance with a context drawn from Old Testament figures like hypostatized Wisdom, the Suffering Servant, the Martyred Shepherd, the Royal Sufferer.

This is not to say that the Bible is given to us principally as a prayer book any more than it is a series of prooftexts for documenting the theses of theological manuals. Sometimes one comes across editions of the Bible with ample annotations "for times of distress/doubt/joy/sorrow/ . . . " One is encouraged to dip in to particular passages in times of need, and such a practice has doubtless been of value to many. Our search for God,

147

however, requires a more consistent attention to his revelation than mere occasional mining of the Scriptures at odd moments; a drama in many acts is being unfolded there, in which we have a part.

Psalms 8, 22, 23, 119, 136

1) Martin Luther thought it was self-evident "why the Psalter is the favorite book of all the saints, and why each one of them, whatever his circumstances may be, finds in it psalms and words which are appropriate to the circumstances in which he finds himself and meets his needs as adequately as if they were composed exclusively for his sake." It seems no accident that the book of the *Psalms*, or Psalter, sits now right in the middle of our Old Testament (which has been arranged differently at different times), interrupting a series of Wisdom books. It is evidently meant for easy access, like any hymn book. Unfortunately, like many hymn books it does not acknowledge the source and liturgical situation from which the psalms have been taken and assembled. And their number, 150, is a suspiciously round one.

   The psalms we have chosen illustrate the different kinds of hymns that the psalms are and their different themes. Basically they are hymns of praise and thanksgiving (like *Pss* 8, 23, 136) and hymns of lament and petition (like *Ps* 22, which we know from its occurrence on the lips of Jesus on the cross). We can imagine individuals singing/reciting them, or a congregation at worship in the case of community lament or praise—the antiphon in *Ps* 136 suiting such a situation. Formally, both types tend to begin and close with similar invocations, the body of the psalm providing the occasion for prayer.

   Ps 119 is out on its own for length; it is a meditation on the Law, each of the 176 verses using some synonym for it. We wonder how Luther would have found it fitting his eulogy of the Psalter.

2) Naturally, a lot of attention has been paid to the *Psalms* by scholars. They insist we see them as liturgical hymns sung to the accompaniment of a stringed musical instrument, so perhaps our modern guitar groups are on target. Some scholars, like Herman Gunkel and Sigmund Mowinckel, have even presumed to specify the particular festivals of the Jewish liturgical calendar in which each type of psalm first found a home. They have been variously numbered in the Hebrew and in the Greek version, so confusion can occur, and they have been arranged in the Bible differently at different times. They are now in five books (like the Torah). The titles heading them are a later addition; David the proverbial psalmist is credited with many, but the psalms derive from various periods: some may even go back to Canaanite origins (*Pss*

29, 93), others are redolent of exile and beyond (*Ps* 137). Not all biblical psalms are in the Psalter, of course—we read Jonah's, for example. Some appear in both Psalter and other books—David's victory song at *2 Sam* 22 appears also as *Ps* 18.

3) We re-read our five psalms, regretting our ignorance of their original musical and liturgical setting, but appreciating the composers' search for God expressed in praise, thanksgiving, appeal, lament, meditation. The serenity of "The Lord is my shepherd" and the long essay on the Law contrast starkly with the (somewhat overstated?) anguish of the sufferer in *Psalm* 22. We note how psalmists are prepared to look beyond individual or national concerns to the beauties of creation as a motif for praise in *Psalms* 8 and 136, though the latter is clearly familiar as well with the well-worn historical surveys of salvation history. While agreeing also with John Calvin, "All the griefs, sorrows, fears, misgivings, hopes, cares, anxieties, in short all the disquieting emotions with which the minds of men are wont to be agitated, the Holy Spirit hath here pictured exactly," we might add the peace and serenity people find in God's love and God's world.

Further reading

O. Eissfeldt, "The Psalter," *The Old Testament. An Introduction*, 444–54

E. S. Gerstenberger, "The lyrical literature," *The Hebrew Bible and its Modern Interpreters*, 409–444

J. H. Eaton, "The Psalms and Israelite worship," *Tradition and Interpretation*, 125–62

Ezekiel 18

1) Just as the *Psalms* reflect community and personal aspects of the search for God, whether joyful or despondent, so this prophet of the Exile seems to be dealing with both national and individual stories of that search. We noted in chapter 9 in considering the development of Old Testament revelation that *Ezekiel* brings a fresh dimension to the problem of responsibility, helping to revise the morality expressed in the proverb known also to *Jeremiah*, "The parents have eaten sour grapes, and the children's teeth are set on edge." Ezekiel takes the story of righteous father, evil son, righteous grandson to drive home his principle occurring also in *Dt* 24.16 of individual responsibility for good and bad conduct (in vv. 5–20). This was good news for those brought up on the current view expressed in the proverb and occurring in several places of the Torah and Prophets.

Next he reinforces the point by treating of an evil person's conversion and a good person's lapse, on the principle, "I have no pleasure in the death of anyone, says the Lord God. Turn, then, and live" (32).

Obviously the prophet had to deal with the objection, "The way of the Lord is unfair"; it was not good news for all. Yet, as Ezekiel was working among the exiles in Babylon, the good news was meant to encourage not just individuals but the nation and allow for return on condition of repentance. The relationship between national and individual search for God is real but more intricate than was supposed.

2) The composition of the book and the dating of Ezekiel's ministry have been subject to much discussion. He provides us with an unusual example of priest and prophet. The mystical and cultic sections of the book also gave pause to those rabbis debating its place in the Hebrew canon, owing to its departures from the Torah. Yet Ezekiel, for his accent on observance of Law, is regarded as the father of modern Judaism. If, as the Talmud says, "*Ezekiel* begins with doom but ends with consolation," our chapter must occur towards the end. Thankfully, it offers no great critical questions.

3) We can read the chapter again from the standpoint of the *reader* considering his or her own search for the God of holiness and appreciating this liberating stance that allows one to live a life in the Lord whose ways are not unfair, and to live with "a new heart and a new spirit" (v.1). Or we can read from the standpoint of the *people* to whom lies ever open a way of repentance and mercy, no matter what the past. The balance between encouragement and warning, to which the Talmud adverts, reminds us somewhat of Jesus' blessings and woes in the Lukan Beatitudes. Both paths lie open to the person and community searching for God.

Further reading

B. S. Childs, "Ezekiel," *Introduction to the Old Testament as Scripture*, London: SCM, 1979, 355–72

S. Terrien, *The Elusive Presence*, 257–61

W. McKane, "Prophecy and the prophetic literature," *Tradition and Interpretation*, 163–88

BIBLICAL TOPIC: OLD TESTAMENT SPIRITUALITY

The Bible has been universally recognized as a great fund of spiritual insights and expressions, and has contributed to people's growth in relationship with God, even beyond the Jewish and Christian communities. So in this sense its spirituality is of a high order. Yet we should recall that it was not composed directly as a treatise on spirituality; it is rather an account of God's dealings with the chosen people in the course of history. So we have no right to be disappointed if the Old Testament does not at all stages measure up to our expectations as a treatise on the spiritual life.

Experience of God

Yet this account of a people's salvation history that is the Old Testament does include individuals' experience of God that can be quite intimate. The vocation of the prophets, like Jeremiah (ch. 1) and Isaiah (ch. 6), and the converse of God with similar figures (e.g. Moses, Elijah) are examples of this spiritual experience. The God they experience is a God who is holy, utterly other: "Holy, holy, holy is the Lord of hosts," the seraphim remind Isaiah in cleansing his lips at his vocation (*Is* 6.3), and Joshua taunts the people with the claim, "You cannot serve the Lord, for he is a holy God" (*Jos* 24.19). This holiness, apartness, which is reflected in cultic and ritual purity, calls for a like holiness in the people: "You shall be holy, for I the Lord your God am holy" (*Lv* 19.2; 20.7; 21.8; 22.9,31). They must keep themselves from uncleanness, or "die in an unclean land" (*Amos* 7.17). Yet holiness is also preparation for involvement in life in society, just as "the Lord of hosts is exalted by justice, and the Holy God shows himself holy by righteousness" (*Is* 5.16).

A range of guidance

The Old Testament also contains much didactic material for religious living by individuals and the community, as we saw in *Ezekiel* and read as well in the Torah, which means "teaching, way of life," and the Wisdom literature. Again we should not be disappointed to find a wide range of inspired guidance, from the merely legalistic and pedestrian, to the fruit of human experience, and at times to the elevated and sublime. Human strengths and weaknesses characterize the composers of this type of composition as much as any other; the spirituality of some sages and legislators does not reach the heights of the mystical experience of the prophets.

Prayers

Prayers in the form of psalms, hymns, oracles appear in the Old Testament in the Psalter and elsewhere. These prayers arise from a range of situations in the community's and the individual's experience of the human and the divine—contemplation of natural wonders, personal misfortune, illness, national success and disaster. Just as Jesus and the evangelists naturally had recourse to Old Testament motifs and prayers, so today our hymns return to these universal spiritual aspirations.

> *These (Old Testament) books, though they also contain some things which are incomplete and temporary, nevertheless show us true divine pedagogy. These same books, then, give expression to a lively sense of God, sound wisdom about human life, and a wonderful treasury of prayers, and in them the mystery of our salvation is present in a hidden way. Christians should receive them with reverence* (Dei Verbum 15).

Further reading
S. Terrien, *The Elusive Presence*, 278–349
I. B. Sloan, "Ezekiel and the covenant of friendship," *BTB* 22 (1992 No. 4), 149–54
R. E. Clements, *The Prayers of the Bible*, London: SCM, 1986

THEOLOGICAL THEME: HOPE, AFTERLIFE

(Be sure to read—aloud if possible—the passages nominated below.)

ISRAEL PLACED ITS HOPE IN THE LORD

From the outset Israel acknowledged that in the Lord lay its hope of prosperity and relief from hardship and enemy assault: "O hope of Israel, its savior in time of trouble," cries Jeremiah (14.8). It is a constant theme in Israel's worship, as the *Psalms* reveal (*Ps* 71.5).

WHO HAD ALWAYS PROVED TRUSTWORTHY

There was ample evidence for Israel that this hope was well grounded: creation of the world, constant fidelity, provision of justice for the oppressed and of food for the hungry (*Ps* 146.5–7). The phrase "waiting for the Lord" is a frequent expression of confidence that the Lord will bring salvation (*Lamentations* 3.25–26).

THAT HOPE LOOKED FORWARD TO NATIONHOOD AND NATIONAL SURVIVAL

The beginning of the patriarchal narrative documents the basis of Israel's hope of becoming, against all hope, a mighty nation and even a source of blessing to other peoples (*Gn* 12.1–3). Yahweh would bring this about, and it was Yahweh—not paltry human allies—to whom Israel should look in time of trouble: so says Isaiah of Jerusalem to king Ahaz, who coyly declines a sign of that continuing assistance (*Is* 7.1–17).

COVENANT BREAKDOWN DASHED THEIR HOPES

But Israel would not always look in the direction of Yahweh, despite covenant obligations to do so, and in consequence they suffered the loss of hope. "We have become orphans, fatherless, our mothers are like widows . . . there is no one to deliver us," cries the author of *Lamentations* (5.1–18).

BUT THERE WAS ALWAYS HOPE OF RENEWED FRIENDSHIP

Yet it was always possible to return to the original intimacy of the close relationship of which Hosea speaks, provided that Israel admitted that its hope lay not in Assyria, chariots and horses but in the Lord (*Hos* 14.1–3).

EXILE WAS A BITTER DISAPPOINTMENT

The greatest national despair was triggered by the loss of the Land of promise: "Behold, we are slaves to this day," admit the people oppressed (*Neh* 9.36). They know they have only themselves to blame, not the Lord (*Ezra* 10.2).

BUT THERE WAS HOPE OF RETURN FOR THE EXILES

"There is hope for your future, says the Lord," Jeremiah tells those who were (or would soon be) in exile; "your children shall come back to their own country" (*Jer* 31.16–17). Second Isaiah too would bring the exiles this same consoling message and exhort them to "wait upon the Lord" (*Is* 40.30–31).

GOOD PEOPLE HOPED FOR REWARD FOR VIRTUE

It was axiomatic of traditional Wisdom that virtue has its own reward in a scheme of things sanctioned by the Lord, a *do ut des* economy: "Honor the Lord with your substance," says an author of *Proverbs*, "then your barns will be filled with plenty" (*Prv* 3.9–10). Job's friends assure him that is what hope means.

BUT GENERALLY NOT FOR LIFE AFTER DEATH

There was nothing beyond this life to look forward to, and so a this-worldly perspective was standard. "Those who go down to Sheol do not come up," says Job, and in this he would be speaking for the Old Testament generally. Isaiah agrees: "Those who go down into the Pit cannot hope for your faithfulness" (*Is* 38.18; *Ps* 88.9–12).

YET SOME CONTINUED TO HOPE AGAINST HOPE

Hope in a future life would not completely go away. We find desperate glimpses in the psalms (*Ps* 73.23–24), in Hannah's prayer ("The Lord brings down to Sheol and raises up": *1 Sam* 2.6), ambiguously in Job (19.25–27).

AND THE OLD TESTAMENT FINALLY HAS A VISION OF AFTERLIFE

It falls to apocalyptic and Greek Wisdom to provide the scenario and the anthropology that can envisage believers living on, once death has claimed them. Seleucid persecution prompts the author of *Daniel* to offer the prospect of resurrection to everlasting life after sleeping in the dust of the earth (*Dn* 12.1–3), while it is Greek philosophy that allows the Alexandrian composer of *Wisdom* to speak of the immortality of the righteous sufferers (*Wis* 3.1–4).

Further reading
B. Lang, "Afterlife: ancient Israel's changing vision of the world beyond," *Bible Review* 4 (1988 No. 1), 12–23
J. L. McKenzie, "Life after death," *NJBC* 1313–14

EXERCISES

1. Can you say, like Luther, that you find some of the *Psalms* so suited to your spiritual needs that they seem "composed exclusively for your sake"? Select some that do seem to speak to you in a particular way.

2. Ezekiel was endeavoring in chapter 18 to deal with the complaint, "The way of the Lord is unfair." How adequately do you think he rebutted it?

3. Are there parts of the Old Testament that are particularly suited to helping us in our search for a Christian spirituality? Think of the popularity today of hymns based on Old Testament motifs.

4. What sort of hope can exist along with a conviction that death is the end of everything? What can the Old Testament possibly teach us about hope?

CHAPTER 13

▼

LOOKING FOR SOMEONE TO COME

texts: *Jeremiah 30–31; 2 Samuel 5–7*
biblical topic: relating Old Testament to New Testament
theological theme: messianic expectations

The books of the Old Testament, the Scriptures Jesus knew, form part of the religious literature of the Jewish people. From the beginning Christians also have read them with care and reverence, and have tried to determine the sense they had for the community of the composers. Clearly Jewish and Christian communities today bring a different world of meaning to their reading of these Scriptures; yet the task of breaking the bread of the Word is similar for both. So in this book we have tried to enter into the mind of the composers, and not foist upon them our own religious world and its traditions. Job and his concerns about an unfair deal, The Deuteronomist moralizing on decline and fall, Second Isaiah consoling the exiles—Jew, Christian and other believers can wrestle with the concerns of these theologians. (We raised this point in chapter 2 as an important question introductory to reading the Old Testament.)

Yet as Christians our biblical canon includes as well another volume, the New Testament. So at some stage the question is going to arise for us: is there a difference in perspective for Christians in looking at individual books and authors within this larger canon? How extensive a pattern of biblical revelation do we see? Does overall significance change, depending on the vantage point taken? Are answers available to New Testament composers regarding critical issues for earlier theologians? Is there now a clearer solution possible for Job's quandary about human wisdom and divine Wisdom? Has the obscurity confronting Old Testament apocalypticists disappeared in the light of a further incarnation of the Word? What difference *does* Jesus make?

So we have left till last the question of the relationship of Old Testament to New Testament, lest it cloud our approach to the Scriptures Jesus knew and prevent our adopting towards them a stance akin to that of his contemporaries. To an extent the issue has arisen in our treatment of

159

interpretation in chapter 11. This particular hermeneutical question, however, calls for individual study.

Jeremiah 30–31

1) Jeremiah was a man who seems to have fallen under that Chinese curse of living in interesting times. Someone in that position would be prompted to ask basic questions about the direction Providence was taking. The northern kingdom of Israel had fallen to the Assyrians a century before he began his ministry in the south, and he lived another forty years to see it too fall to invaders, despite his best efforts to achieve some national reconciliation. These chapters are rather difficult to follow, with some oracles suggesting a place in the early years of his ministry and others presuming exile of the south has already begun. Some offer hope to Israel ("Jacob shall return"), some to Judah, some to both.

   The most remarkable of the loose collection of oracles is that which forecasts that the Lord will make "a new covenant with the house of Israel and the house of Judah" (31.31–34), which John Bright in his commentary calls "one of the profoundest and most moving passages in the entire Bible." The term "new covenant"—which Jesus will quote—occurs nowhere else in the Old Testament. In what sense is it a new covenant, and the old abrogated? The key seems to lie in its observance: "I will put my law within them, and I will write it on their hearts," the Lord says. The newness lies with the people, set in their sin, and their capacity to observe the covenant. This novelty is a theme we remember from Jeremiah's contemporaries Second Isaiah and Ezekiel.

2) The ordering of oracles in prophetic books is often haphazard, hardly chronological. The chronology of Jeremiah's life and the sequence of the book's chapters are likewise obscure. The authenticity of various sections has also been disputed, as has the role of Jeremiah's secretary Baruch in composition. There is also the question of similarity to Second Isaiah, involving perhaps dependence on the part of either prophet. Our chapters seem largely to be directed to Israel, though those key last few verses include Judah as well and may be a separate oracle.

3) Despite Jeremiah's proverbial reputation as a prophet of doom, in rereading these particular chapters we appreciate the forward-looking perspective and the promise of restoration, especially for the north. The phrase "Jacob shall return and have quiet and ease" in fact seems, in hindsight, to be an unduly sanguine forecast. The encouragement of

"Do not be dismayed, I am with you" certainly reminds us of Second Isaiah. And it is particularly the house of Israel to whom the promise of a new covenant written on the people's hearts is made. We wonder if, when Jeremiah died in Egypt around 587, he felt disillusioned. Judah by then was also on the way to exile.

Further reading
S. Terrien, *The Elusive Presence*, 253–56
L. D. Davis, "Jeremiah: prophet doomed to strife," *TBT* 26 (1988 No. 2), 104–112

2 Samuel 5–7

1) David and the Davidic dynasty are central to Old Testament and New Testament thought. We noticed in chapter 6 how Deuteronomist and Chronicler differ in the degree to which they are prepared to admit David's weaknesses along with his strengths. But even The Chronicler could hardly take exception to the David who appears in these chapters, cementing his political position in north and south; securing a center of empire in Jerusalem; coping with the Philistines; developing his own family as distinct from Saul's line; being anxious for the cult through ark and even temple—the though latter was postponed; showing humility and gratitude in prayer, song, dance. The chapters culminate in the oracle of the Lord via the prophet Nathan. Through word play on "house" there emerges some ambiguity about David's role in building a *temple* but none about the Davidic *dynasty*. This dynasty is now no longer a suspect institution (as *1 Sam* 8 suggests) but an eternal kingdom: "Your house and your kingdom shall be made sure forever before me; your throne shall be established forever" (7.16). The New Testament, of course, will likewise relish these chapters.

2) It seems that the Deuteronomistic history around the time of the Exile has welded together blocks of material about David in the two books of *Samuel*, such as the prophecy of Nathan, the relocation of the ark, David's attempts to secure his position. The origins of the various blocks are not identical, so views expressed on the temple and the institution of monarchy do not always cohere. These three chapters of *2 Samuel* certainly bear the marks of an attempt to legitimate the Davidic dynasty, even extending to closing down the line of Saul through Michal's punishment. The centerpiece is the oracle of Nathan (who, we are told, otherwise rarely appears) and its promise of perpetuity for the Davidic and Solomonic throne. James W. Flanagan remarks of it, "This unit is fundamental in Israelite, Jewish, and Christian royal messianism" (*NJBC*

156). The Chronicler would have been proud of it (and in fact incorporates a similar version of the oracle, *1 Chr* 17, as do *Pss* 89 & 132.)

3) We appreciate in our re-reading what is occurring in the narrative, how David and his line are being firmly established, blessed by God and generally glorified—free of any negative commentary at this stage by The Deuteronomist. In this light, otherwise puzzling incidents, like the severe punishment meted out to Uzzah for touching the ark and Michal for ridiculing the dancing David, make some sense. Political and military successes and the heavy accent on cult promote the same theme. The climax is quite glorious, the perpetuity of the Davidic line being repeated over and over—and this at a time when monarchy and other institutions were being swept away in the chaos. A long perspective was required of The Deuteronomist's readers, which the New Testament will provide in the figure of another anointed ruler.

Further reading

A. F. Campbell, *The Study Companion to Old Testament Literature*, 190–213

R. Alter, *The Art of Biblical Narrative*, London-Sydney: Allen and Unwin, 1981

BIBLICAL TOPIC: RELATING OLD TESTAMENT TO NEW TESTAMENT

As we have often noted, the Scriptures known to Jesus and his early community of followers were those of the Old Testament, though other religious writings were circulating at that time as well. This community eventually developed its own scriptures without forfeiting its claim to the earlier religious compositions as a record of their experience of God. *2 Peter* 3.15–16, a relatively late work, mentions Jewish and Pauline scriptures in the same breath. The apologist Justin, in debate with Jews in the second century, reasserts this claim for his community; and the Christian Bible ("Book") continued to include both bodies of scripture, customarily referred to on the basis of biblical usage itself as Old Testament and New Testament.

Promise and fulfillment

The precise relationship of the two collections was a matter of keen study and debate from the beginning. Jesus himself is on record as requiring of his disciples a proper understanding of earlier Scriptures in relation to himself (*Lk* 24, *Jn* 5). The Jewish evangelist Matthew set a trend of recognizing a pattern of promise and fulfillment, quoting texts of the Old Testament to present Jesus as their fulfillment. The Fathers would find this an adequate statement of the relationship; Augustine's dictum became classic, "The New lies hidden in the Old, the Old is made clear in the New."

Type and antitype

We noted in our treatment of interpretation (ch. 10) a further development of this approach to relating Old to New. The theological school of Alexandria, originally a great Jewish center of learning in Egypt, developed the system of *typology* for finding significance in certain Old Testament events and figures in the light of their New Testament counterparts. Thus Isaac and the Passover became for these exegetes (perhaps with scriptural encouragement) types, imprints, outlines of future realities: Jesus and his Paschal Mystery (the antitypes). A problem with such a hermeneutical approach is that it enables us to relate only a fraction of the Old Testament to the New.

The mystery of Christ

A more comprehensive approach to the relationship is that of Paul the Jew, who looked back on the Old Testament history and Scriptures and on their New Testament continuation, and saw there a pattern or "mystery" in Old Testament, apocalyptic terms, which he called the mystery of Christ. Within this overall pattern, which "gathers up" (Greek *anakephalaio*, Latin *recapitulo*) all things human and cosmic (*Eph* 1.10), Jesus comes at the focal point. The Fathers of East and West, like Maximus and Irenaeus, would continue to speak of such a divine plan in terms of *anakephalaiosis, recapitulatio*. Such a hermeneutical pattern allows us to see all Old Testament events and figures occurring within a divinely guided mystery.

> *We continue to use the expression Old Testament because it is traditional (cf. already 2 Cor 3.14) but also because 'Old' does not mean 'out of date' or 'outworn.' In any case, it is the permanent value of the Old Testament as a source of Christian Revelation that is emphasized here (cf. Dei Verbum 3). Our aim should be to show the unity of biblical revelation (Old Testament and New Testament) and of the divine plan, before speaking of each historical event, so as to stress that particular events have a meaning when seen in history as a whole from creation to fulfillment. This history concerns the whole human race and especially believers. Thus the definitive meaning of the election of Israel does not become clear except in*

the light of the complete fulfillment (Rom 9–11), and election in Jesus Christ is still better understood with reference to the announcement and the promise (c.f Heb 4.1–11).

From Notes on the correct way to present the Jews and Judaism in preaching and catechesis in the Roman Catholic Church, *Vatican Commission for religious relations with the Jews, 1985*

Such an approach as Paul's to interpretation also has the merit of allowing us to relate the Judeo-Christian scriptures and their peoples' experience of God to those of other religions, though Paul and the Bible generally are not interested in doing that, and are perhaps not aware of other peoples' scriptures and history. Eastern religions had achieved great advances towards an opening to the transcendent in the first millennium before Jesus, not to mention the Aborigines' 45,000 years of residence in Australia. All such developments occurred within the mystery of Christ, even if not registered in our necessarily blinkered Bible.

Further reading

R. C. Hill, *Jesus and the Mystery of Christ*, ch. 3

B. Griffiths, *A New Vision of Reality*, London: Fount, 1992

J. Jensen, "The Old Testament in the New Testament and in the Liturgy," *TBT* 28 (1990 No. 4), 207–212

THEOLOGICAL THEME: MESSIANIC EXPECTATIONS

(Be sure to read—aloud if possible—the passages nominated below)

ISRAEL'S SALVATION ALWAYS LAY IN THE LORD'S HANDS

Through thick and thin Israel always believed that salvation lay with the fortress and the rock that was the Lord. Yahweh would see them through all troubles and make them prosper. Even in the Torah a royal dimension is lent to this hope; Jacob's song in *Genesis* 49 speaks of the scepter always belonging to Judah. In the eighth century Isaiah of Jerusalem sees the Lord intervening to act as judge and peacemaker (*Is* 2.2–4).

THIS SALVATION WAS SEEN AS MORE MATERIAL THAN SPIRITUAL

Though it was the Lord who is king, his rule and his interventions would result rather in material, even political, benefits than a purely spiritual reign. The exiles in Babylon, for instance, expect of the Lord, through Cyrus the anointed (*messiah* in the Aramaic form), something tangible by way of release and vindication; and they are promised "the wealth of Egypt and the merchandise of Ethiopia" (*Dt-Is* 45.14).

NATIONAL SETBACKS FOCUSED HOPE ON FUTURE SALVATION

A series of setbacks and disappointments for north and south gave a longer perspective to expectations of salvation. What seemed conquered, possessed, settled could be snatched away. Then the people could only hope for a future restoration, and looked for signs of its coming, like the sign Isaiah offers the north (*Is* 7.14).

PROPHETS, PRIESTS AND KINGS WERE ANOINTED FOR THIS ROLE

While Israel took a long time to develop a notion of a definitive Messiah, many figures were anointed to perform a share in the salvific work. Prophets were anointed for their task (*Ps* 105.15); so too were priests (*Lv* 4.3). Kings in particular were anointed to act in the place of Yahweh, to rule justly, as David was (*1 Sam* 16.6).

A SERIES OF SALVIFIC FIGURES WERE LOOKED TO

Amongst all these anointed figures, certain ones were particular objects of a hope that they might intervene decisively on behalf of Israel: Elijah, a prophet-like-Moses, Son of Man.

NONE OF WHOM WOULD BE A SUFFERING OR A DIVINE MESSIAH

Unlike the New Testament's presentation of Jesus, the Old Testament has no suffering messiah, nor a divine Messiah.

ANOINTED KINGS WERE SEEN AS SAVIORS SENT BY GOD

After initial ambivalence about kingship, and despite northern suspicions of a Jerusalem dynasty, kings were eventually seen as being anointed to act on Yahweh's behalf, saviors sent by God. So says the oracle we just saw in The Deuteronomist, and which was also recorded by *1 Chronicles* 7 and *Psalm* 89: "Righteousness and justice are the foundation of your throne . . . our shield belongs to the Lord, our king to the Holy One of Israel" (vv. 14,18).

THE KING WOULD RULE JUSTLY AND SAVE THE POOR AND NEEDY

Despite evidence to the contrary and the warnings of some traditions, Israel had high expectations of its king in terms of salvation: "May he defend the cause of the poor of the people, give deliverance to the needy, and crush the oppressor" (*Psalm* 72.4).

LATER, A SUCCESSOR TO DAVID WAS THOUGHT ESSENTIAL

Since in fact not all kings did measure up to expectations, popular hope came to envisage a king of the line of David as the one who would bring salvation. Isaiah sees this successor as recipient of the spirit of the Lord, and romanticizes the effects of his reign, even to wolves living with lambs (*Is* 11.1–9). Micah, too, sees salvation coming from Bethlehem (*Mic* 5.1–3).

DESPITE LOSS OF THE MONARCHY, A SHOOT WOULD CONTINUE

The disappearance of the Davidic line could mean the failure of these high hopes. Yet Jeremiah is confident a righteous branch of that line will be raised up to reign as king and deal wisely (*Jer* 23.5–8). Ezekiel, too, speaks of a sprig remaining (*Ez* 17.22).

YAHWEH WOULD ACT THROUGH A SUPREME KING, *THE* MESSIAH

With no likelihood of restoration of monarchy, hope became even more desperate and the perspective lengthened. Post-exilic prophets like Zechariah encourage the people to look forward to a king coming to Jerusalem, his dominion from sea to sea despite his riding on a donkey

(9.9–10). Even if he is hardly regal in appearance, Yahweh rules through him definitively.

Further reading

R. E. Brown, "God's future plans for his people," *NJBC* 1310–12

E. Rivkin, "Jewish Messiah," *IDB Supp* 588–91

B. W. Anderson, *The Living World of the Old Testament*, 187–88, 589–91

EXERCISES

1. The term we find in *Jeremiah*, "new covenant" (new "testament" in its Latin translation), is obviously very significant for Christian readers, especially as it is unique in the Old Testament. Does Jeremiah seem to have a clear insight into what the new covenant/testament will involve? Are we clearer, or as clear?

2. Read again the oracle of Nathan in *2 Sam* 7, and then compare it with the attitude to monarchy expressed in *1 Sam* 8. How do you account for the difference?

3. Have you personally developed an adequate understanding of the relationship of the Old Testament to the New? Can your theology incorporate the whole extent of the Old, and as well avoid a pejorative attitude to it?

4. There are some loose ideas about the Old Testament's expectations that go under the name *messiah, messianism*. Are you sure your understanding is supported by the text of the Old Testament? Express your ideas precisely.

CHAPTER 14

DIRECTIONS OF FURTHER STUDY

The hope is that study of this text thus far has helped promote a meeting with the Word in his incarnation in the text of the Old Testament. As a go-between, it can now drop from sight, the reader being in a position to delve more deeply into the riches contained in the Scriptures Jesus also found nourishing. There are books that the previous chapters did not delve into, like *Ezra* and *Habbakuk*, even if referred to briefly for theological themes. Other such themes, too, could be highlighted. There is a lot more that could with profit be studied of the historical, cultural, geographical contexts of the Old Testament to broaden our understanding. This chapter will just point in the direction further study might take when opportunity allows—not for the beginner but for someone now feeling comfortable with this vital component of our tradition.

LITERATURE BEYOND THE CANONS

We have made the point from the outset that the religious composition available to the devout reader in Jesus' time was not identical in extent to the present Hebrew Bible, nor even the later larger collection accepted as normative by the Christian communities. Despite the technological difficulties of literary composition compared with our times, and the relative rarity of suitable materials, believers of all colors and convictions put into writing their creeds and theologies, some startling even today when we can number a great range of such speculation. As well, there were the compositions of earlier, exotic cultures like those of Egypt and Mesopotamia, Canaan and Phoenicia, not to mention the classical civilization of Greece, that had left their imprint on Israel's cosmogonies, proverbs and theodicy as found in canonical texts. So we should not get the impression that the Bible stands alone and unique in its world as a religious monument. We might turn to those other bodies of religious writing so as to contextualize the Old Testament scriptures and thus better appreciate its significance, originality and eventual influence.

Other cultures

Our map of the Near East in the biblical period (p. 4) and commentary on it highlighted the peculiar position of Israel in the Mediterranean and in the Fertile Crescent that left it vulnerable to both depredation and also influence of a political, economic, religious and literary kind. Prophets like Isaiah and Hosea warned of this contiguity, yet there is no doubt that Israel's literature, if not religious practice, benefited from it. Deuteronomist and Chronicler make mention of the ways in which Temple building capitalized on foreign resources; likewise creation accounts and covenants, proverb makers and psalmists could find in the polished works of Egypt, Assyria, Babylon, Canaan, Phoenicia, Ugarit and Mari medium and inspiration for telling Israel's own story. Modern commentators on *Genesis* and *Exodus, Judges* and *Kings, Psalms* and *Proverbs, Job* and the latter prophets refer frequently to echoes in the biblical text of the Epic of Gilgamesh and the Code of Hammurabi, a Hymn to Ishtar and the Instruction of Amen-em-Opet, the Words of Ahiqar and the Babylonian Theodicy. (All of these are conveniently reproduced for us in *ANET*, which has become a vade mecum for any biblical commentator.) We are as grateful for this literary fertilization as we are for the *pax Romana* that contributed to the spread of the Word after Jesus' time.

Israel's other literature

As we shall see when looking at the rise of rabbinic tradition in the next chapter, from the time of Ezra there developed within Israel itself other religious composition than Torah, Prophets and Writings. Beyond the body of oral Torah that grew up with rabbinic commentators, a parallel line of composers began the production of religious works often modelled on biblical books or characters, such as Enoch, the patriarchs, Elijah, Solomon, Job, Isaiah, Jeremiah, Baruch. This line of literary work continued well into the Christian period, and it often becomes unclear whether we are reading an original Jewish work, a Jewish work reshaped by Christians, or a specifically Christian composition. The original language is often also not clear, whether Hebrew or Greek.

Predictably, authorship of these works is usually pseudonymous. The various books of *Enoch* dating from as early as the fourth century, and therefore much older than some of our canonical Old Testament, are the work of unknown authors, though the *Book of Jubilees* from this body of literature accredits that popular figure from primeval history with the invention of writing. The New Testament (*Jude*) quotes the Enochic books. The Fathers in some cases took them seriously, and even Augustine thought him a reputable author as distinct from much circulating then under his name. So this body of religious composition goes under various names: *pseudepigrapha*, though we know much canonical material likewise bears the name of a character other than the true author; *apocrypha*, though this term is ambiguous in reference, including at least in Protestant usage the deuterocanonical books, a different corpus; *intertestamental*, which at least has the merit of allowing for a lengthy period of some six or seven hundred years spanning both testaments.

Despite their apocryphal character, these books exercised a great influence on the New Testament, on the Fathers of the Church in the following centuries, and on the development of Christian theology. *The Testaments of the Twelve Patriarchs* we now know to be of Jewish-Christian origin from the first or second century after Jesus, but it was thought by its influential editor R. H. Charles to be much earlier. It found its way into all the textbooks and was required reading for students of the New Testament until recently. Today a critical reader finds it moralistic and misogynist.

Much of the other material in the intertestamental books apes biblical Wisdom and apocalyptic writings, but usually falls short of the biblical model. Both the *Psalms of Solomon* and the *Odes of Solomon* are sapiential in character; but a gnostic flavor has crept in, a dualism being apparent between truth and falsehood, light and darkness. Likewise, in chapter 42 of *1 Enoch* wisdom is hypostatized as in canonical *Proverbs* and *Sirach*, but significantly, unlike them, it shows this Wisdom figure not prepared to live on earth: "Wisdom did not find a dwelling, she returned to her place and took her seat in the midst of the angels." A highly developed angelology, also as in gnostic writings, has left its mark on Christian theology, too.

(A handy modern collection of intertestamental books is by H. F. D. Sparks, entitled somewhat misleadingly, *The Apocryphal Old Testament*.)

Literature from Qumran

One advantage to us of our knowledge of this further Jewish literary material is the realisation that the Bible does not give us the only window onto Palestinian Judaism and early Christianity, that they are not univocal but diverse movements, that the canons are not an adequate picture of the religious world of the times. A further such reminder came with the discovery this century of the body of literature from Qumran on the north-west cliffs of the Dead Sea, the product of a Jewish splinter group that had taken up residence there around the mid-second century. Dating is much argued, involving the relation of the group to Christianity, for one thing; recent advanced radiocarbon dating has tended to suggest an earlier date.

The find included biblical manuscripts, valuable for their antiquity and ability to shed light on the accuracy of our later texts, commentaries on biblical texts, and a range of literature composed by the community for its self-regulation and theology. This community, like Jesus and his contemporaries, knew a wider range of biblical material than is found in the Hebrew Bible, as well as those intertestamental works mentioned above.

The non-biblical compositions of the Dead Sea, such as *The Community Rule* and *The Damascus Rule*, reveal a highly organized, very observant, liturgy-conscious sect (Essenes perhaps, or Sadducees) of Palestinian Judaism distinct from the middle ground of the rabbis, and distinct again from the reform to which Jesus called his fellow Jews. The movement did not survive the Roman onslaught of 70. Editor of the scrolls, Geza Vermes, says of it: "Animated by the loftiest ideals and devoted to the observance of 'perfect holiness,' it yet lacked the pliant strength which enabled orthodox Judaism

A section of the Isaiah scroll discovered in 1947 in Cave 1 at Qumran.
From a century or two before Jesus' time, it contains ch. 53.1–9, part of the fourth Song of the Suffering Servant, which the early Church loved to apply to Jesus: "Surely he has borne our infirmities and carried our diseases . . . ".
While resembling our present Hebrew text, it also reveals the antiquity of the LXX.
(Printed with permission)

to survive." It does underline once again, however, the wide literary pool in which other Jewish composers worked and from which a canon was eventually selected.

Gnostic literature

One of the features of the Dead Sea material that distinguished it from orthodox Judaism, including our Old Testament texts, is the *dualism* we found also in some intertestamental literature. The scrolls set up a dichotomy between knowledge, truth, grace on one side, and error, evil on the other; between a Prince of Light and an Angel of Darkness. These oppositions we recognize as *gnostic*, and associate more readily with that vast body of literature and array of movements that proliferate a century after Jesus under the inspiration of figures like the Jewish platonist philosopher Philo and the Christian from Alexandria, Valentinus. Their difference from those other branches of Judaism, rabbinic and Christian, can be seen by comparing *The Gospel of Thomas* with the canonical Gospels possibly contemporary. The former were characterized by dualistic and docetic tendencies rejected by the early Christian community, as the New Testament itself says. The same is true of the gnostic creation myth. It developed in opposition to the biblical version, considered overly material; we find it in *The Apocryphon of John*.

Once again they illustrate the diversity of the literary world of Judaism and early Christianity, lest we think these authors did their composition in a religious and literary vacuum. We would do well to savor these extrabiblical works of the period, the better to appreciate the Old and New Testament texts we accept as authentic tradition.

Further reading
J. B. Pritchard, *ANET*
H. F. D. Sparks, *The Apocryphal Old Testament*, Oxford: Clarendon, 1984
M. McNamara, *Intertestamental Literature* (OTM 23)
G. Vermes, *The Dead Sea Scrolls in English*, 3rd edn, Penguin: Harmondsworth, 1988
B. Layton, *The Gnostic Scriptures*, London: SCM, 1987

LEARNING A BIBLICAL LANGUAGE?

The story is told of a professor at an English university in the old days (when no women attended) who habitually commenced his classes on the Hebrew language with the words, "Gentlemen, this is the language God spoke." One wonders how many, including himself, believed him. There certainly can be a mystique surrounding the biblical languages—Hebrew, Aramaic, Greek—that leaves the ordinary reader of the Bible feeling at the mercy of linguists and translators, being unable ourselves to read biblical texts "in the original." There is no cause for concern, however, since today with the rapid dissemination of scholars' work any faulty translation, let alone sleight of hand, would be rapidly pounced upon and thus bring the translator into notoriety. As we said in chapter 1 in dealing with modern translations, there is a wide range of good translations of biblical texts in literally thousands of modern languages readily available, thanks to the wonderfully zealous Bible Societies.

This is not to say that time put into learning the biblical languages by us modern Westerners is time wasted: where would we be without the great linguists who have brought us the Scriptures in translation? Beyond the work of providing communities of believers with accessible translations, there is the considerable advantage of being able to catch every nuance of the biblical composer's thought in his own medium of expression. There is the proviso, of course, of being sure we have his work in a reliable text. We would need the further skills of paleographers, textual critics, even archeologists to be utterly sure of that. How many skills can one puny reader aspire to?

As Raymond Brown says of a scholar's responsibility, "Some familiarity with the structure and thought patterns of these languages is essential for a type of professional biblical knowledge"; but as for the rest of us, "With English as one's only linguistic tool, it is possible to have a good knowledge of the Scriptures" (NJBC 1149–50).

So what should we set ourselves as a realistic goal after achieving a basic familiarity with the Scriptures Jesus knew? (What languages in fact did Jesus himself know?) It is good for us to know something in general of the family of languages named "semitic" after Noah's son Shem by German scholars. Beyond Hebrew and Aramaic this group includes Canaanite, Phoenician, Ugaritic and Syriac in the north-western branch and Arabic in the southern. Whatever the divine familiarity with Hebrew predicated by the English professor, it is the language learnt by the Israelites from the Canaanites when they came into contact with them.

The influence on biblical Hebrew of more ancient forms has been brought to our attention by great linguists like William Albright and Mitchell Dahood. The latter cites the illuminating instance of discoveries this century at Ebla in the north-western region (see our map, "The Near East in the biblical period") in connection with the puzzling phrase in *Genesis* 1 about human beings made in God's likeness—*demuth* in biblical Hebrew—and their consequent responsibility to manage the rest of creation.

This consequence has always puzzled exegetes. Dahood shows that in lists of deities discovered at Ebla there occurs a word in that more primitive semitic language, *dimutu*, which is related to the biblical word. So we can now see the Priestly composer viewing the human being as a deputy of the Creator and thus divinely charged with stewardship of creation.

Aramaic, as we saw, was increasingly in use by the biblical people on return from Exile, and bulks large in the books of *Ezra* and *Daniel*. As the language of Jesus, it is important for scholarly study of the New Testament. There have been those who claimed that the Gospels were composed originally in Aramaic, but scholars like Matthew Black and Joseph Fitzmyer have discredited that theory, though the former would like to trace sayings of Jesus to an Aramaic original. The Greek of the New Testament is marked by many "Aramaisms", usages of the one language accommodated in translation into the other.

> *Four languages were to be found in first-century Palestine:* **Greek** *was the speech of the educated 'hellenized' classes and the medium of cultural and commercial intercourse between Jew and foreigner;* **Latin** *was the language of the army of occupation and, to judge from Latin borrowings in Aramaic, appears also to some extent to have served the purposes of commerce, as it no doubt also did of Roman law;* **Hebrew***, the sacred tongue of the Jewish scriptures, continued to provide the lettered Jew with an important means of literary expression and was cultivated as a spoken tongue in the learned coteries of the Rabbis;* **Aramaic** *was the language of the people of the land and, together with Hebrew, provided the chief literary medium of the Palestinian Jew of the first century.*
>
> Matthew Black, An Aramaic Approach to the Gospels and Acts, *3rd edn, Oxford: Clarendon, 1967, 15*

There is a painting by an Old Master of St Jerome at work in his cave on the study of the Bible. Jerome, from modern ex-Yugoslavia, settled at Bethlehem, and gave himself to learning Hebrew and translating the Old Testament. In the painting he is seen to be finding this heavy going; of the learning of Hebrew (Aramaic, Syriac . . .) it could be said, in Shakespeare's words, "Knowledge hath a bloody entrance." Jerome, of course, went on to leave us with a complete Latin version of the Bible "for common use", *Vulgate*.

Do we really see ourselves engaging in scholarship at that level? Acquisition and retention of those linguistic skills will involve much labor and constant use if the flower so sorely grown is not to wither on the vine. Perhaps we could settle for acquiring a basic grasp of Greek script so as to be able to recognize key New Testament words and even use a basic resource like Kittel's *Theological Dictionary of the New Testament* (abbreviated *TWNT*). Beyond that, there are good grammars for biblical

Hebrew and biblical Greek; and the generous Bible Societies will even provide classes with Hebrew Bibles and Greek New Testaments *gratis*.

But before taking the task on, think of St Jerome, and of the many resources for Bible study in English of which we may not yet have taken advantage.

Further study

P. Auvray et al., *The Sacred Languages*, ET London: Burns & Oates, 1960

W. D. Stacey, "The languages of the Bible," *Groundwork of Biblical Studies*, London: Epworth Press, 1979

J. J. M. Roberts, "The Ancient Near Eastern environment," *The Hebrew Bible and its Modern Interpreters*, 75–86

J. Barr, *The Semantics of Biblical Language*, Oxford: OUP, 1961

————— "Semitic philology and the interpretation of the Old Testament," *Tradition and Intepretation*, 31–64

THE WORD BEYOND THE BIBLICAL WORLD

From the outset in this book we have tried to set the Word of God as our goal; the textual form of the Word is a derivative thing, if the most accessible form in most cases. So in our Old Testament, and in the New, we recognize the presence of the Word. In the predominantly Christian circles in which we move, at least literary and academic circles, what we select for study from the ancient world comes down largely to the Scriptures Jesus knew, though we have also suggested the literary world of his time was rather wider than these suggest. What still remains to be acknowledged, if we are to contextualize these Jewish and Christian Scriptures adequately, is the vast body of religious literature of other world religions, largely Asian religions. The Word has been active throughout history and the world, not just in our story and our communities.

The word beyond Christianity

The narrowness of our focus does not do us credit as disciples of the Word, nor does it respect the breadth of focus of Christians in the early centuries after Jesus. Though they had few of the advantages we enjoy for accessing other peoples and their religions and literatures, the early Apologists strove to recognize and uphold the activity of the Word in Christianity and beyond. Justin Martyr, Clement of Alexandria, Theophilus of Antioch, the great Origen in the second and third centuries developed a theology that would see the Word active, not only in Jesus and the scriptures of his followers, but in other communities and their literatures. Theophilus wrote a Christology for his pagan friend Autolycus that makes no mention of Jesus, only the Word. Clement sees the Word active also in the Hebrew prophets, in the Sybilline prophetess, in the classical poets Pindar, Aeschylus, Sophocles, Euripides. As Augustine tells us in the *Confessions*, even his pious mother, St. Monica, insisted he have a good education in the pagan classics so as to make him a better Christian.

A great religious movement

What these admirably comprehensive theologians were not aware of, as we are, is the great body of religious composition emanating from religious communities much more antique than Christianity and even Judaism strictly speaking. The various forms of Hinduism, Buddhism, Taoism, Confucianism, Zoroastrianism trace their origins to a period at least as remote as the return of the exiled community of Judah from Babylon, from the beginnings of Second Temple Judaism. In fact, among the Hindu scriptures the Vedas and the Brahmanas go back to the time of the Exodus or centuries before; the Upanishads are closer to the time of the early great Greek philosophers like Heraclitus and the Hebrew major prophets. These scriptures emanating from Asia, as well as those Jesus and ourselves have come to know, demonstrate an opening, a great religious breakthrough to the transcendent in that millennium before Jesus. We are inclined through our ignorance to confine such breakthroughs to the religious cultures we are familiar with.

The Buddha and the scriptures that enshrine his teachings, the Tripitaka, also go back to midway through the first millennium before Jesus. Persian and Chinese scriptures are similarly ancient and similarly significant. No wonder Vatican II speaks affirmingly, in the manner of Justin in the second century, of the seeds of the Word to be found germinating in these non-Christian religions. Much later come the scriptures of the Muslims who form the world's most numerous religious group—unless we lump all Christian groups together. Muslims reverse the Koran (Qur'an, "recitation") as the Word of God transmitted to Mohammed through the angel Gabriel. About as lengthy as the New Testament, The Koran contains snippets of Old and New Testaments, *mishnah* and *midrash*, and Zoroastrian scriptures (*Avesta*).

"Oral scripture"

Of course, there is only so much an interested reader of the world's religious traditions, or better a disciple of the Word, can reach. Still, while coming to meet the Word in the Old Testament, we should not be unaware of the activity of the Word so generously documented beyond its pages. And this not simply in so many other religions' scriptures. Think of the unwritten stories of many peoples' religious history, their traditions of God's dealings with them, that remain as "oral scripture" in cultures that have retained a living oral tradition.

Further reading

M. Eliade, *The Encyclopedia of Religion*, New York: Macmillan, 1987

A. Hiltebeitel, "Hinduism," *The Encyclopedia of Religion*, vol. 6, 336–60

F. E. Reynolds, "Buddhism: an overview," *The Encyclopedia of Religion*, vol. 2, 334–51

F. Rahman, "Islam: an overview," *The Encyclopedia of Religion*, vol. 7, 303–372

B. Griffiths, *A New Vision of Reality*, ch. 3

FOLLOWING AN AREA OF INTEREST

This is a book, not for specialists but for beginners, who nevertheless will hopefully develop a taste for individual study of the Old Testament. Jesus encouraged his listeners, especially those who thought their traditions had no place for him, to "search the Scriptures" and arrive at a fuller understanding of them. That presupposes in us a basic familiarity with them, having overcome the physical barrier and arrived at an appreciation of the overall theological message of the Old Testament and the drift of individual composers. Access to the wide range of biblical resources and informed commentators should also have been achieved at this initial stage.

Then one is equipped to look for individual trees among a wood which is no longer uncharted. The word "research" is sometimes lightly used to mean any kind of elementary enquiry, whereas at least in biblical studies a truly professional researcher would require knowledge and skills such as the biblical and perhaps other modern languages, the elements of textual criticism, literary analysis. Not all of us can conduct research in the technical sense; mostly we depend on the professional scholars to mediate the fruits of their research to us, and hence we have concluded each section of this text with references to such further reading.

Reading around any topic should make us eventually independent of an elementary guide such as this, ready and interested to take our study further, if not to become a fully-fledged researcher. In chapter 1 we have surveyed the resources available for study of the Old Testament, from Introductions to concordances and dictionaries and so to individual commentaries. We have taken account of the literary context in which Old Testament texts arose, and have seen something of their linguistic diversity. So we are unlikely to take any false directions if we head off in search of some information when a question takes our fancy, and we should know where to turn to get satisfaction.

In wanting to get beyond an elementary grasp of the Old Testament we are responding as well to what learning theory has to tell us of the dimensions of knowledge of a subject. Educationists point out that there are stages beyond *content knowledge*, factual information, organizing principles, central concepts; the present text has provided this basic knowledge of the Old Testament, for instance. *Substantive knowledge* of a discipline includes explanatory frameworks or paradigms that are used both to guide inquiry in the field and to make sense of data. In biblical studies the adoption of a critical approach so as to obviate fundamentalism would fall under this head. *Syntactic knowledge* includes an awareness of the ways in which new knowledge is brought into the field. The movement from historical to canonical criticism in Old Testament study would be an example of this, and we should know something about it. Educationists also point out that, in addition to these dimensions of knowledge, the *beliefs* of the teacher or student come into play—such as our conviction expressed in the introduction and manifested in the structure of the text that a theological approach is basic to understanding the Old Testament aright.

A practical example

At Easter we usually hear some rendition of Handel's *Messiah*, where the well-known libretto takes an excerpt from *Job* 19.25–26:

> For I know that my Redeemer lives,
> and that at last he will stand upon the earth;
> and after my skin has been thus destroyed
> then in my flesh I shall see God.

We are asked, and we ask ourselves, how this apparent glimpse by Job of life beyond the grave and bodily resurrection sits with the general agnosticism of the Old Testament on the subject (as treated in elementary fashion in our theological theme "hope, afterlife" in chapter 13). How do we go about pursuing this interesting detail?

First, we read Job's sentiments on the subject elsewhere in the book, in the first and second cycle of speeches (14.14–17; 17.13–16) and in his finale (30.23). Generally we would have to say from the book as a whole that Job has no firm hope of personal resurrection. We return to our pericope in chapter 19, and re-read it, looking at the *NRSV* footnotes, (not feeling able to deal with the critical apparatus provided in the Hebrew Bible.) The translator/editor suggests so many alternatives to readings in those verses, or admits so often that the meaning of the Hebrew of a verse is uncertain, that we realize we cannot build too much on this one pericope in isolation.

We turn to our commentators, who should be able to tell us what the Hebrew does mean, and why the text is unreliable. The *Anchor Bible* commentator, Marvin Pope, laments that the text of the book is the "most vexed in the Old Testament." Another, M. Barré, suggests an emendation of the text of our pericope to read:

> *I know that my redeemer can restore life/health,*
> *and that my guarantor can raise from the dust.*

We read more about the role of a *go'el*, redeemer, that we had met in *Ruth*. The *OTL* commentator, Norman Habel, rehearses all the textual complexities and is inclined to deprive Job (and Handel) of any break-through into a vision of resurrection: "This verse is notoriously difficult . . . The suggestions are endless. It seems best, especially in view of the literary design, to link v. 26a with the preceding verse and simply recognize that Job believes his defender will rise at the end to plead his cause even though his skin has peeled off in death" (*Job*, 293.) We feel let down, but also in good hands.

We turn to a series of journal articles on *Job*, and find they prefer to ignore the remarkable implications of this apparent exception to the Old Testament's silence on afterlife, or seize on other intriguing features of the book such as the relation of the prose to the verse sections, or just admit the impossibility of depending too much on any part of a suspect text, as does Terrence W. Tilley: "At crucial points, the text of the book is so indeterminate that the 'text' of *Job* is, to a significant extent, made, not found" ("God and the silencing of Job," *Modern Theology* 5 [1989 No. 3], 258.)

So, as a result of our further study, we have reached several enlightening conclusions. One is a general one: verses quoted out of context can be misleading. Another is more specific: 19.25–26 cannot safely be taken at face value, whether we compare them with Job's other statements in the book or try to evaluate the condition of the text. A further general conclusion is: a thorough, evaluative commentary (like Habel's) is invalu-able for those of us lacking the specialist skills a good commentator can command. In short, we now feel we are on solid ground in disallowing Handel's invocation of Job in the sense he does - not that this will spoil anyone's enjoyment of the *Messiah*.

FURTHER CRITICAL APPROACHES

In chapter 4 we looked at a range of skills, techniques and approaches adopted by students of the Old Testament to reach an evaluation, or "criticism", of those texts that Jesus knew and that we want to get to know well so as to meet the Word there. Failing to adopt such by now well-honed skills and thus reading biblical material "uncritically" would result in the reader's treating it like any current writing and failing to appreciate the differences. Fundamentalists fall into that trap, as we saw.

A window on the world

Thus scholarship in recent centuries developed branches of *historical criticism* so as to gain a window on the world of the Old Testament, its authors and redactors who were responsible for composition orally and in writing and the community/ies for whom they composed, their situation and concerns. It was that world and those literary agents that were at the focus of attention in such studies; the text itself was but a window opening on to them (see table, p.185). Much attention has been paid to The Deuteronomist's account of Solomon's accession in *1 Kings*, we saw, not only for a more factual account of that event than The Chronicler's, but for an insight into the theological analysis of a redactor shaping earlier material to find a message for his community in the light of impending disaster centuries later. What that redactor, or any author, intended was an important element in determining the text's meaning.

Such critical techniques, beyond eroding a fundamentalist approach to texts like creation stories and a prophetic narrative like *Jonah*, have helped us appreciate how the Word spoke to communities at the time of composition, how Hosea's listeners were alerted to the danger of relapsing into Canaanite fertility cults, how disillusioned communities after the Exile were questioning previously certain verities in the words of Qoheleth and the author of *Job*. In recent times *sociology* has also shed light on the make-up and situation of the communities to whom the text was directed. We gained a lot from these critics' attention to the world behind the text. Jesus was closer to that world than we are, and we need to work hard at it.

Focus on the text

Such criticism by biblical scholars, though classed by them as "literary", tended to adopt an historical focus, as its name suggested, and concentrated less on features of the text itself than is true of literary criticism generally these days. *New criticism*, in fact, is prepared to ignore the intention of the author of a literary work and focus on the text itself, which now has a life of its own, as is true particularly of Old Testament texts, whose authors have long gone and have perhaps had their efforts reshaped by others, as in the case of Hosea, Ezekiel and the oracles of prophets generally. These critics would find meaning predominantly in the text as we read it off the page. We can, for instance, recognize the careful patterning in chapter 1 of *Genesis* without having to know anything of the Priestly composer and his historical situation. However, historical criticism in fact would suggest that a different composer takes over only in chapter 2, verse 4b. So it is not quite productive to ignore authorship completely, as such *structural criticism* tends to do.

We can understand the appeal of new criticism to students of the Bible, who sometimes found that scholarly detail robbed them of the magic of a text (who wants to know if a dozen redactors/editors can be detected in the book of *Ecclesiastes*?). The Word speaks to us now in the completed text as we find it within the covers of our Bible, not in atomized particles. So, thanks to scholars like Brevard Childs, readers were encouraged to apply another approach (called by some *canonical criticism*): not to break up the text but to treat it as a literary and theological unit and even part of the larger unit, the whole canon in which a passage or book now occurs and which speaks to the faith community.

The songs of the Suffering Servant, for example, whatever their referent at the time of composition, now occur within the whole work of Second Isaiah, itself contained within the book of *Isaiah*, which in turn stands within the whole Hebrew Bible. And in our Christian Bibles, New Testament authors gave those songs a further significance. A full grasp of the songs' meaning, therefore, is certainly not achieved only by returning to their original *Sitz im Leben* ("life situation"; see Glossary). In fact, the text and its composer(s) speak and have spoken to a succession of faith communities, it seems.

A mirror reflecting the world

Further developments in biblical criticism and hermeneutics—since the search is for meaning—have seen the focus move further from author to text to canon and on to reader. *Reader-response criticism*, or *contextual criticism* (there is a variety of terms used), sees the text as a mirror reflecting a world into which the reader is invited (Sandra Schneiders), in other words, we look at the Exodus, not as historical event but as liberating experience for us too. Literary criteria are employed to see how a text, or its oral original, appealed to original audience/readers and can appeal to us today (*rhetorical and narrative criticism*). Other contextual critics examine how today's readers, from their particular viewpoint, which can be sectional or partial, are affected by aspects of the Old Testament, positive or negative. Feminist critics, for example, highlight the attention women are given in such books as *Ruth* and *Esther*, or the neglect of a woman's sensitivities such as we found in the patriarchal viewpoint in *Judges*. Liberation theologians show how a reader's oppressed situation can promote a response to accounts of oppression in the Bible.

Approaching the text of the Old Testament

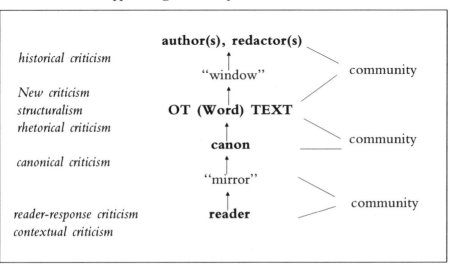

If our aim is to have the Word in the pages of the Old Testament speak to us, then these further skills, techniques, approaches are of value. To all these many critics, then, as to the biblical authors, belong the title "servants of the Word." We should benefit from their service as we are able.

Further reading

J. Barton, *Reading the Old Testament. Method in Biblical Study*, London: DLT, 1984

R. C. Culley, "Exploring new directions," *The Hebrew Bible and its Modern Interpreters*, 167–200

S. Schneiders, "Hermeneutics: The contemporary situation," *NJBC* 1158–62

J. S. Kselman, "Modern Old Testament criticism," *NJBC* 1127–29

B. S. Childs, *Introduction to the Old Testament as Scripture*, chs 1–3

APPENDIX 1

WHAT'S IN A NAME?

Right from our Introduction we encountered difficulties with the traditional terminology *Old Testament*, giving us reason to adopt the alternative *The Scriptures Jesus Knew*. One was the unfortunate "churchy" term *testament*, not found in normal English usage and not clearly tracing its roots—through Latin, Greek, Hebrew—in the fundamental notion being conveyed of the *relationship* the Lord wants to form with his people. Another challenge was to use a title that implied *all* the Scriptures that Jesus knew, and that we want to read to meet the Word fully there, not merely those in our present Hebrew Bible (see above p.xvi and ch. 3). We have come to see there has been ambiguity about the contents of the Old Testament, Jewish and Christian.

A further contemporary problem with the traditional terminology is that people can take offence at *Old* Testament if it is understood to mean God has forsaken a relationship with one community and replaced it and them with another. That was not the sense intended when the New Testament itself came up with this terminology, with the encouragement even of the Old: cf. *Jer* 31.31–33 and the reflection on that passage in *Hebrews* 9 and 10; also *2 Cor* 3. Still, the possibility of misunderstanding leads some people to suggest instead terms like *Hebrew Scriptures/Christian Scriptures, First/Second Testament*. Those engaged in Jewish-Christian dialogue reflect this sensitivity, and a journal like *Biblical Theology Bulletin* honors it in its editorial policy.

The trouble is that these alternative terms themselves are not free of ambiguity or the whiff of discrimination. The Scriptures Jesus knew were in fact not all in Hebrew; some were in Greek and Aramaic. *Jewish Scriptures* would at least be accurate. *Hebrew Bible* too is a clear reference to the rabbis' limited selection of texts after Jesus' time. From earliest times, as we have seen, the Christian community adopted for themselves all the Scriptures Jesus knew, not confining themselves to the yet unformed New Testament—so they all rightly sit within the covers of our Christian Bible.

A practical educational difficulty with using an alternative to *Old Testament* is that our libraries are full of books and journals using the traditional and not necessarily discriminatory terminology, which we also feel free to use here while being sensitive to the concerns of others looking

189

for an alternative phrasing. That the matter is not an issue with most scholars was made clear in 1990 with the publication of two major works of scholarship: the *New Jerome Biblical Commentary* continues to speak of Old Testament and New Testament, while in the lengthy introduction by Bruce Metzger to the *New Revised Standard Version* of the Bible this issue was not one of the many touched on as coming under review.

For further discussion of the question and the issues involved, see R. W. L. Moberly, *The Old Testament of the Old Testament,* Minneapolis: Fortress, 1992. An alternative phrasing he cites for Old Testament/New Testament, "The Scriptures"/"The Apostolic Writings" (from P. Van Buren), also suggests the appropriateness of a title like *The Scriptures Jesus Knew*. Joseph Jensen discusses the issues in connection with the traditional usage in the new *Catechism of the Catholic Church* "Beyond the literal sense. The interpretation of Scripture in the *Catechism of the Catholic Church*," *The Living Light* 29 (Summer 1993) 57–58, reaching the same conclusion.

APPENDIX 2

▼

WORD AND TEXT: RABBIS, TALMUD

W e have stated the purpose of this text as facilitating a meeting between the believer and the Word of God. As Isaiah reminds us, the Word has been spoken for such a purpose, and will not return fruitless (*Is* 55.11). Already in that speaking, the Word has taken human form and is perceptible by us; our creed in fact refers only to such divine activity: "He has *spoken* through the prophets (= the inspired authors of both testaments)." Yet most of us generally think of the Word in its textual, biblical, scriptural incarnation, a further stage in divine communication, *koinonia*. We are inclined to read the Word rather than listen, even in the liturgy when the Word is proclaimed for our attention; and admittedly the availability and convenience of the printed Word encourages that—unlike Old Testament times when such means of communication were much rarer. Perhaps today technology is turning the wheel around to its original point of making the spoken Word more easily accessible to us, in the liturgy and for private meditation.

Word spoken and written

So we are coming to appreciate that the Old and New Testament Word is primarily an oral communication. Apart from the assistance of technology, literary critics, anthropologists, even biblical scholars are highlighting this truth: that the Word of God mediated to us through Jeremiah or Moses or the psalmists is (like Shakespeare, as every schoolboy knows) not marks on a page but a sound for recital, for action, *drama* in the original sense of that word. Amos heard it roaring like a lion (3.8), Joel too (3.16), and neither mentioned rushing to put it in writing. In fact, the written word is rarely referred to in Scriptures composed when the necessary skills and materials were not readily available (cf. *Jer* 36; *Is* 30.8).

Anthropologists are discouraging us from feeling superior to cultures for whom "scripture is not merely the written book, but the word that is chanted, sung, danced about, meditated upon, devoutly copied, recited in rituals, enacted in pageantry and drama"—as Cassian Agera says of the tribal religions of north-east India; they have "liberated scripture from its dead letter" and from "the silent hegemony of the eye alone."

This is making the biblical scholars take account of "the orality of scripture" a term Walter Ong tells us has been made necessary by our failure to develop concepts to deal with oral art forms. They are going back to texts to find there hardly concealed clues to the basically oral character of the material. Yehoshua Gitay finds in examining Second Isaiah that the author "designed his material to be heard; he tried to appeal through the ear." We remember that in the Torah the Word is a creative event, *dabar*, in itself; we recall that *Deuteronomy* tells us that it is by that Word issuing from the mouth of God that we live (8.3). In the following appendix on "Pentateuchal criticism" we will see literary critics assailing a well established Document Hypothesis for the formation of the Torah because it is too textually oriented, not taking sufficient account of oral transmission of traditions before fixed written texts were arrived at.

Not surprisingly, then, the New Testament can speak of the Old Testament Word in its pristine oral form even when employing conventional terms like "scripture," Greek *graphe*. So Peter to his community:

> First of all you must understand this, that no prophecy of scripture is a matter of one's own interpretation, because no prophecy ever came by human will, but men and women moved by the Holy Spirit spoke from God (2 Pet 1.20–21).

So too the author of *Hebrews*:

> In many and various ways God spoke of old to our fathers by the prophets (1.1).

And the early Fathers can be quoted for frequent similar references, like Origen on the harmony of all these expressions of the Word:

> The whole of Scripture is but one single instrument of God, perfect and harmonious, which renders one harmony from different sounds for those willing to learn (In Ev. Matt. 2).

The bishops at Vatican II, mostly Western, had to be reminded of this by an Easterner in their discussion of the Bible: "Scripture is a prophetic and liturgical reality; it is a proclamation more than a book" (Neophytus Edelby, titular archbishop of Edessa).

From word to text

Yet, despite this now widely lost sensitivity to the credal insistence on the spoken Word, there is evidence of the Jewish and Christian communities' anxiety to hold on to it as far as possible while having also to settle for a text of the Word to ensure adequate transmission. In the case of the latter community our evidence is largely about the composition and transmission of the Gospels. The historian Eusebius of Caesarea records at half a dozen places in his *Ecclesiastical History* accounts of earlier commentators from the second century onwards which frequently indicate reluctance by the evangelists and Paul to commit their message to writing. One such account, indebted to Origen, says these ministers of the Word "gave little consideration to care in composing written words. And they did this because they were serving a greater and superhuman ministry" (*E.H.* 3,24) that is, the preaching of the Word. He also reports Papias still earlier endeavoring to get word of the Lord from living witnesses for the reason that "I did not suppose that information from books helped me so much as that from a living and abiding voice" (*E.H.* 3,39).

There is clearly here suspicion of a textual form as being derivative; it is a *theological* concern, that the spoken Word is more vital than the written. These Fathers' intuition is supported by modern hermeneuts like Paul Ricoeur and Hans-Georg Gadamer, who point out that a text gains a life of its own once it is cut loose by its author, who can no longer control it—just the fear Peter seems to have had (in Eusebius's further account, *E.H.* 6,14) in authorising a version of his preaching that becomes Mark's Gospel. This theological concern about movement from word to text is generally omitted from consideration by the many scholars who have studied the process, including Birger Gerhardsson, Rudolf Bultmann, Werner Kelber, who tend to think of the process in terms of canon, technology, rhetoric.

Gerhardsson gets closer to the theological issue when he makes a comparison with Jewish practice, namely, the rabbis' struggle against the written transmission of the oral Torah, the body of commentary on the Torah that had grown up over the centuries. This reluctance he puts down to "a commonplace which we recognize from elsewhere in antiquity: an attitude of scepticism to the written word. The idea is stressed—not least in the school tradition—that what can be learned from the written page cannot be compared with that which may be learned from the lips of a living person" (*Memory and Manuscript. Oral Transmission and Written Transmission in Rabbinic Judaism and Early Christianity*, 197). He could also have cited the Roman moralist Seneca: "The living voice will help you more than the written word" (*Ep. Mor.* 6,5).

Torah written and oral

To what is Gerhardsson referring in mentioning rabbinic practice and the oral Torah? That takes us back to that critical moment, the destruction of Jerusalem and the Temple with it, and the exile of the community of

Judah. The monarchy disappeared and, at least for the time being, Temple worship. Ezekiel, the father of modern Judaism, who is in Babylon with the exiles, records his meeting (8.1; 14.1; 20.1) with the elders of Judah to discuss the situation and what might be done. In lieu of Temple and throne they had for their guidance, above all, the Torah, that encapsulation of divine Word and human articulation that had always served as a model for the community. From such meetings for prayer and instruction there developed a class of skilled commentators and instructors in Torah, *sopherim*, "scribes". When the community returned to Jerusalem they had such men to guide them, pre-eminently Ezra, "a scribe skilled in the Law of Moses" (*Ezra* 7.6). His role: "Ezra had set his heart to study (*darash*) the Law of the Lord, and to do it, and to teach the statutes and ordinances in Israel" (7.10).

The particular style of commentary on the Torah indicated by Ezra's study of it thus came to be known as *midrash*, a close textual investigation, akin to what we know as *exegesis*, that yielded far more than a superficial reading might suggest. "The sacred words became an inexhaustible mine which, when quarried, produced rich treasures of religious and ethical teaching," says A. Cohen. We can see within the Old Testament itself a late author like Ben Sira conducting just such an investigation and reworking of the text of *Genesis* 1 (*Sir* 16.24–17.17) in his role as rabbi, or teacher—the first to inform us definitely that schools operated for the purpose. Such *midrashic commentary* on biblical books could be more oriented to law and prescription, called *halakah*, or to lore and narrative, *haggadah*.

A synod or Great Assembly of teachers developed in Ezra's time, known as *Knesseth*, the name taken today by the Israeli parliament. Later it developed into a body with a Greek name, *synhedrion*, which took a Hebrew form as *Sanhedrin*, a body we know also from New Testament times, composed of priests and laymen. The former were more sympathetic to Hellenism and the written Torah, the latter opposed to Greek influence and insistent on the value of an oral Torah which was the further commentary that provided "a fence around the Torah", in the words of a great rabbinic commentary, *Pirke Aboth*, Sayings of the Fathers. The New Testament knows both groups as Sadducees and Pharisees, respectively. Since the former were clerical, associated with Temple worship, the destruction under the Roman general Titus in the year 70 meant their demise. The influence of the Pharisees in such matters as fixation of the canon of the Hebrew Bible was uncontested. (This also explains their relatively "bad press" in the New Testament.)

Mishnah and Talmud

Alongside the *midrashim* of the rabbis in the synagogues there thus developed in this period of early Judaism at the hands of another group of scholars, the Tannaim, a body of "teaching", *Mishnah*. It was largely oral in character, for reasons mentioned above. It was characterized by two schools of interpretation, one founded by Hillel that was lenient in interpreting the Law, the other founded by Shammai. Pharisees were divided at the time of Jesus by their loyalties to one school or the other. Eventually the *Mishnah* had to be codified in some written form; this was done by Rabbi Juda ha-Nasi, "the prince," "the saint," around two hundred years after Jesus. To it "additions," *Tosefta*, were made, and eventually a body of further "study," *Gemara*—compiled by the Amoraim in rabbinic academies of Palestine and Babylon in the third to the sixth centuries of the Christian era—was included as well. All this constitutes the *Talmud* ("study"), which thus occupies in Judaism an authority inferior only to the Torah itself on which it is a living commentary: words upon the Word. Talmudic literature embraces all these bodies of commentary, including the *midrashim*.

Thus the Word of God, which Christians know as the Old Testament, continued in Judaism to receive an investigation and commentary that we

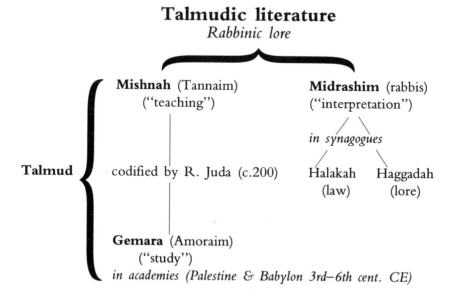

Talmudic literature
Rabbinic lore

Mishnah (Tannaim)   **Midrashim** (rabbis)
("teaching")   ("interpretation")

                              in synagogues

Talmud   codified by R. Juda (c.200)   Halakah   Haggadah
                                          (law)   (lore)

Gemara (Amoraim)
("study")
in academies (Palestine & Babylon 3rd–6th cent. CE)

Tosefta is "addition" to the Mishnah

know as Talmudic literature, rabbinic lore, of various kinds over the many centuries of the growth of Judaism out of the disaster of the Exile. Jesus the Jew knew it and made a contribution. The Christian community, of course, developed its own commentary and extension of this Word, which for various reasons took also a textual, scriptural, biblical form.

Further reading

W. A. Graham, *Beyond the Written Word. Oral Aspects of Scripture in the History of Religion*, Albany: UNY Press, 1989

W. Ong, *Orality and Literacy. The Technologizing of the Word*, London-New York: Methuen, 1982

B. Gerhardsson, *Memory and Manuscript. Oral Transmission and Written Transmission in Rabbinic Judaism and Early Christianity*, Lund: Gleerup, 1961

A. Cohen, *Everyman's Talmud*, New York: Shocken Books, 1975

R. C. Hill, "From Good News to Holy Writ: the share of the text in the saving purpose of the Word," *Estudios Biblicos* 51 (1993), 145–62

APPENDIX 3

PENTATEUCHAL CRITICISM

Earlier in our text we looked into the general question of biblical criticism (ch. 4), and have done some reading of texts from those five books that constitute the Torah. (The word "penta-teuch" referred originally to the five jars in which scrolls would have been kept.) We also noted how important the Torah has been for Judaism. Remember Jacob Neusner's definition: "the whole body of belief, doctrine, practice, patterns of piety and behavior, and moral and intellectual commitments that constitute the Judaic version of reality." It was the same for Jesus, who speaks frequently in our Gospels of "the Law" (a Greek New Testament phrase for it), or "Moses," its reputed author. So it is understandable that it has come under the close scrutiny of biblical scholars from the outset. We have seen the rabbis making it the object of their commentaries and thus amassing a parallel body of "oral Torah" that also became normative for the community. Jesus had something to say about that practice, too.

Moses as author

So, despite the great reverence for this key body of religious literature, critical readers of the Pentateuch put to it the kinds of questions normally addressed to other great compositions—about its authorship and process of composition, date and place of origin, and the way to interpret it, as they would with the work of Shakespeare or Homer or Virgil, or even the other great religious compositions in world history. Taken at face value, the Torah is the work of Moses, who tells of Israel's election and foreshadowing in the lives of the patriarchs, who leads them out of slavery into the wilderness, where God appears to them and forms a close relationship with them, and where Moses addresses lengthy discourses to them as they prepare to enter the promised land of Canaan without him. He dies in its closing pages. A preface is appended linking this story to the origins of all peoples and the world.

But already early this millennium some rabbis themselves were asking if Moses could be author of a whole work that not only recounted his death but also seemed to repeat and contradict itself at times. Christian scholars in the sixteenth, seventeenth and eighteenth centuries felt less religious inhibition in posing such questions and looking at the wider question of pseudonymous authorship in the Old Testament, which affected also Solomonic authorship of Wisdom material and Davidic authorship of psalms. They addressed a series of problems about Mosaic authorship of the Pentateuch:

> *repetition*: two accounts of creation, two genealogies of Cain, two flood stories, two incidents, of Sarah at risk, two stories of Hagar and Ishmael, two theophanies at Bethel, two versions of the Decalogue.
>
> *contradictions*: sacrifice to be offered on one altar only (*Dt* 12.13–14) or on many altars (*Ex* 20.24); flood waters remained for 40 days (*Gn* 7.17) or 150 days (*Gn* 7.24)
>
> *different names:* Mt Sinai/Mt Horeb; Canaanites/Amorites;Yahweh/ Elohim.
>
> *different styles/tones*: morally sensitive/morally crude; God remote/God close; people fearful/people bold.

Such phenomena, not peculiar to the Pentateuch in ancient oriental literature, were susceptible of various explanations. The favored one became known as the *Document Hypothesis*, and is associated with the name of Julius Wellhausen in the ninteenth century. It proposed that four written documents had been composed by different authors in the period from the monarchy to the exile (J "Yahwist", E "Elohist", P "Priestly", D "Deuteronomy"), gradually coalescing into the present text without removing all signs of original composition. The characteristics and style of each author could be demonstrated beyond simple adoption of one name for God (in the case of Yahwist and Elohist). They each had their own theology and theological theme: an accent on blessing in the Yahwist, on fear of God in the Elohist, on the Land in the Priestly composer, on law in Deuteronomy.

Such an approach to the composition of the Pentateuch, which informs most of recent Old Testament textbook material, reduces the role of Moses to original inspiration rather than active literary author. As such it would not be acceptable to orthodox Judaism or those Christians who are impatient of modern critical techniques. Even among scholars it has been found to do scant justice to the process of tradition of original material and to oral transmission in particular. There is also the problem that documents like J and E, singly or combined, seem not to be known to other Old Testament composers in the period after the monarchy. Even the patriarchs do not figure much in pre-exilic composition.

A form of the Document Hypothesis

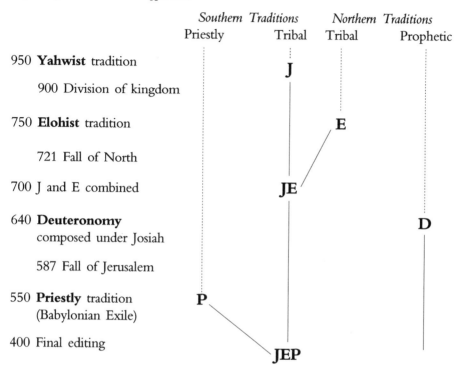

	Southern Traditions		Northern Traditions	
	Priestly	Tribal	Tribal	Prophetic
950 **Yahwist** tradition		**J**		
900 Division of kingdom				
750 **Elohist** tradition			**E**	
721 Fall of North				
700 J and E combined		**JE**		
640 **Deuteronomy** composed under Josiah				**D**
587 Fall of Jerusalem				
550 **Priestly** tradition (Babylonian Exile)	**P**			
400 Final editing		**JEP**		

Pentateuch as a whole work

Today the movement in biblical scholarship is away from the atomizing tendency that once characterized historical criticism and towards a synthesizing attitude that concentrates on the completed work and the community for whom it came together, without denying the presence of earlier sources/traditions/ strands. Accordingly, we are looking again at the Pentateuch as a whole work rather than at its parts, while allowing also for signs of multiple authorship. One such revisionist critic, R. N. Whybray, writes: "However we conceive of the date, identity and purpose of the final author, redactor or editor of the Pentateuch, his notion of a literary work did not include a concern for such modern literary concepts as consistency of thought or smoothness and unity of style: the Pentateuch in its final form is concrete proof of this. The existence of such varied material cheek by jowl was evidently entirely congruent with his notion of a history" (*The Making of the Pentateuch*, 238).

Such revisionist critics would place the final version of the Pentateuch around the time of the Exile and would accord a major role to the Deuteronomistic historians who were responsible for that other great work, the Former Prophets, as well as the book of *Deuteronomy*. They thus accept the work of earlier German giants in the field, Gerhard von Rad and Martin Noth, who on the basis of *Dt*'s distinctiveness debated whether to see a literary movement that stretched from *Genesis* to *Joshua*, thus making of it a Hexateuch, or rather see *Dt* beginning the other historical work, thus leaving a Tetrateuch.

It would therefore be good for us to re-read what we noted in chapter 6 about the theological character of Old Testament historical writing lest we adopt a fundamentalist interpretation of the Pentateuch.

Further reading

D. A. Knight, "The Pentateuch," *The Hebrew Bible and its Modern Interpreters*, 263–96

R. E. Clements, "Pentateuchal problems," *Tradition and Interpretation*, 96–124

R. E. Murphy, "Introduction to the Pentateuch," *NJBC* 3–7

R. N. Whybray, *The Making of the Pentateuch* (*JSOT Supp.* 53), Sheffield: JSOT, 1987

APPENDIX 4

▼

BIBLICAL WISDOM

Fashions change in biblical scholarship, as has just been made clear in looking at the Pentateuch. Attention to Wisdom material is another glaring example. A few decades ago, when the great German tradition critics like Gerhard von Rad were in the ascendancy and nothing that did not center on Old Testament historical traditions was thought worthwhile, Wisdom was the poor relation in biblical study, Old Testament and New. To Von Rad it was "slightly tinged with the pallor of theological reflection. We look in vain for clear evidence of the direction of this scheme of history towards a definite historical hour with whose concrete situation Israel had to identify herself." We have now come full circle to what might seem *a pan-sapiential approach*: all kinds of biblical material are seen to have come under the influence of the sages, and in the New Testament Jesus as Wisdom in person appears everywhere.

A wisdom perspective

To avoid going to extremes ourselves, we need to be clear as to what Wisdom is. The Christian Bible lists a range of books among "Poetry and Wisdom," including *Song of Songs* and all the *Psalms*. We saw in chapter 13 that in fact psalms are of all types, only a few sapiential. (The name "sapiential" comes from the Latin *sapientia*, wisdom.) The books of *Proverbs, Job, Ecclesiastes, Wisdom of Solomon, Sirach* are normally nominated as Wisdom books. Are there any others? If the proverb is thought to be the basic sapiential literary form, then no other books are; but we saw in chapter 8 that these days a whole range of literary types are thought to be sapiential and are to be found elsewhere in the Old Testament. In fact, *Wisdom*—which is concerned with a lot more than wisdom, the quality of being wise—is not so much a matter of form, literary type, but of perspective. Roland Murphy, a prolific writer on Wisdom, says, "Wisdom is both content and style" (*NJBC* 447); it is perhaps better to think of it as a worldview, "an approach to reality" (Murphy elsewhere), a "way of thinking" (Von Rad), "neither a similar theological purpose nor a fixed literary genre but rather an identifiable intellectual stance and literary idiom" (E. H. Heaton).

207

Wisdom's many faces

What constitutes this distinctively Wisdom perspective, as distinct from a prophetic perspective or an apocalyptic perspective? There are many characteristics or aspects that go to form it. Von Rad noticed, in the passage from his *Old Testament Theology* we quoted above, that the traditions it draws upon are less historical, less tied into Israel's story than social and generally human. The proverbs that recite conventional wisdom never mention the patriarchal figures that loom large in the Torah; they draw on what people generally have found to be true. It is people, human nature, human behavior that the sages are interested in, to the disgust of the tradition-historians. Yet the anthropology of Wisdom is not an "us versus them" anthropology, dividing people into Jews and Gentiles, but good and evil people, wise and foolish—universal categories. It is not that the sages are unaware of Israel's history; large slabs of *Sirach* (chs 44–50) and *Wisdom* (more than half, chs 10–19) retrace this history, but from the viewpoint of the gift of wisdom to key figures. And not simply exemplary Jewish figures like the patriarchs but as well people from universal history, Adam and Enoch and Noah. Wisdom is quite sexist, however: only male figures appear.

The universalism of Wisdom will recommend it to the New Testament, and expands the Old Testament's parochialism.

Unlike much of the Old Testament, Wisdom does not draw its knowledge from divine revelation, the Word of the Lord, like the Deuteronomistic history or the prophets. Its epistemology depends on experience; Qoheleth knows that everything is futile because he has found it to be so, the proverbs of Solomon formulate the fruit of the same experience and, like Ben Sira, communicate it to others less wise. Its morality, too, rests not on a Sinai epiphany and legislation but on what people have experienced in life—though Job has to tell his friends that they must be honest about this and not come up with a piously fictitious interpretation of experience. "The tents of robbers are at peace," he reminds Zophar, who would like him to think that his own suffering must *a priori* be due to evildoing. No, the true sage is definitely an *a posteriori* moralist, reasoning from experience of the real world.

The real world also involves people in social relations, in human converse and dealings with the wise and foolish, rich and poor, young and old, and Wisdom has much to say on this matter. It is not concerned with the interaction of the major political forces of the day, even if these have led to national crises provoking a radical questioning of verities, as is evident in *Job* and *Ecclesiastes*. Yet there is sufficient mention of king and court to lend color to king Solomon's patronage of Wisdom skills mentioned in the

Former Prophets. What does strike us about biblical Wisdom, as also extrabiblical Wisdom found in intertestamental, gnostic, Qumranic texts, is its misogynism: the loose woman is a constant threat if *Proverbs* is to be believed. Qoheleth may "have found one man among a thousand, but a woman among all these I have not found" (7.28). Yet the quality of wisdom, hypostatized stunningly in *Proverbs* 8 and *Sirach* 24, is a woman— thanks to the influence of foreign goddesses? This is a figure the New Testament will love to see realized in Jesus.

Wisdom universal and cosmic

The universalism of the sages extended beyond their interest in people, all people, to include the whole material universe. They are not confined in a pattern of Yahweh's dealings with his people, in the manner of a Yahwist or Deuteronomist, but uniquely take a serious interest in creation and show an affinity with it. Only such a naturalist could depict the role of Lady Wisdom in creation that at least three of the books do, or like Qoheleth speak so poetically and pathetically of the ageing process in terms of nature (*Eccl* 12). There is a refreshingly materialist, this-worldly, cosmic viewpoint in Wisdom that we find in the psalms and creation stories, where the hand of the sages has also been detected. Solomon himself is credited with just this interest and affinity in "speaking of trees . . . animals and birds, reptiles and fish" in composing his three thousand proverbs (*1 Kgs* 4.33)—as, of course, did Jesus, who knew well and quoted from Old Testament Wisdom.

So it has to be admitted that Wisdom is not primarily religious, other worldly; it is solidly secular, even if Ben Sira and the author of the prologue to *Proverbs* have been subject to sacralizing influences. It is not concerned with the cult, sacred places, sacred times, sacred people. Its interest is not in the angels and heavenly visitants that people intertestamental and gnostic literature. This is not to say that Wisdom is not theological, but that it has a distinctive theology. Its God is certainly not the God of the patriarchs but a universal Providence interested in the welfare of all people and things. Its salvation history is not one people's but that of the whole universe. It is not so much interested in dogmas but in morality, in reward and punishment rather than truth and error (unlike the gnostics).

Job finally realizes that divine Wisdom, not human wisdom, is reflected in an "unfair" world. So its theological themes are not election and deliverance, covenant and infidelity, but good and evil, suffering and prosperity—universal, human concerns found in the literatures of all peoples.

Those tradition historians who would prefer a canon within the canon of the Old Testament are affronted by this breadth of focus, as also by the resemblance to similar material from Egypt and Mesopotamia, Canaan and Phoenicia, to which Israel's Wisdom is clearly indebted (as a glance at *ANET* will reveal).

Such is the distinctive perspective of biblical Wisdom, its worldview; it is not simply a matter of "content and style." It would be inadequate to focus on the literary characteristics of Wisdom, like proverb and parable, as some have - especially as today scholars are attributing to the sages a huge range of literary types, from fable and allegory to hymn, exhortation, even torah, as we noted in chapter 7. As a later sage, Jesus, demonstrates, Wisdom has much more to offer us than that. Old Testament Wisdom gives us a window on God's world that prophecy, history, apocalyptic do not provide, and that we today especially need.

Further reading

J. A. Emerton, "Wisdom," *Tradition and Interpretation* 214–37

J. L. Crenshaw, *Old Testament Wisdom. An Introduction*, Atlanta: John Knox Press, 1981

R. E. Murphy, "Introduction to Wisdom literature," *NJBC* 447–52

C. H. Scobie, "The place of Wisdom in biblical theology," *BTB* 17 (1984 No. 2), 43–48

R. C. Hill, "The perspective of Wisdom," *Scripture Bulletin* 21 (1991 No. 2), 16–20

APPENDIX 5

▼

OLD TESTAMENT THEOLOGY

Having read thus far, you will find it obvious that this book's primary focus in reading Old Testament texts is on *theology*, not on *history*, or *religion*, or even on *faith*. To promote a meeting with the Word in these texts can only be a theological exercise essentially; readers are helped to see what the authors, human and divine, are saying that is relevant to communities and listeners/readers, both at the time of composition and today. You might wish to read that introductory section again (pp. xvii) to see the reasoning behind this focus on theology in a guide to the Old Testament. It explains also why each chapter has spent time examining a theological theme that was at the forefront of many authors' attention at different periods, like the choice of the people, their deliverance, their relationship to God and fidelity to commitment. And the biblical texts chosen for each chapter were selected and examined primarily for their theological significance, even if this was done in context.

Biblical theology

Thus, theological emphasis in our text is quite obvious. What is not so obvious is what the term "Old Testament theology," or even "biblical theology," means. Sometimes we speak of biblical theology in the sense of the biblical character that good Christian theology should have, conceding that theology has not always been done with a dependence on one of the basic traditions of the community, the Scriptures, the Bible, the Word of God incarnate in this form, as it should have if it is to be authentic. John Calvin made clear what the Reformers thought of the role of the Bible in this regard: "Let this be a firm principle: No other word is to be held as the Word of God, and given place as such in the church, than what is contained first in the Law and the Prophets, then in the writings of the apostles; and the only authorized way of teaching in the church is by the prescription and standard of his Word" (*Institutes of the Christian Religion*). Vatican II put it equally forthrightly in *Dei Verbum* for the Catholic community, telling its theologians that scriptural study is "the soul of theology," as previous popes had insisted.

In fact, that is *not* the sense of Old Testament theology intended here.

213

We are looking at the theology that emerges from the Old Testament, the understanding that comes to faith as the composers achieved it. We studied a great number of Old Testament theologians wrestling with contemporary problems and feelings and challenges to see how faith spoke to them—theologizing, in other words. The Deuteronomist seeks an explanation of Israel's and Judah's fall from grace and loss of nationhood. The Yahwist finds his people's origins and others' related in the divine plan. Jeremiah and Second Isaiah and Ezekiel try to read the meaning of national disaster for its victims. Psalmists trace beauty and success and pain and sickness back to a Provident God. Sages struggle to make sense of good and evil. All were believers, and all theologians, and their faith and theology speak to us as it did to their listeners.

Listening to the composers

We have to be good listeners, too, if we are to gauge the drift of their theologizing. The concerns are primarily their concerns, not ours; we cannot bring interpretations and requirements of ours to issues affecting them. Our theological manuals may list categories, largely abstract and speculative, that seem to serve our needs, whereas The Chronicler focuses on the needs of the restored community in fifth or fourth century Jerusalem, and the author of *Maccabees* is concerned about Hellenistic influence and pressure upon Jewish ways, as are the authors of *Daniel* and *Judith*. We may not, as some have done, impose some theological schema of our making on the Old Testament, such as God-Man-World, and think we are doing justice to a Word we are not even listening to.

Old Testament theology is not like a medieval system, where a Thomas Aquinas felt free to adopt a pattern from neoplatonic philosophy and build his system around it from the many theses he wanted to incorporate. That is not biblical theology in any sense of the word; we know the Old and New Testaments much better than the Angelic Doctor did.

And if we are to listen to the theologians of the Old Testament as they expose their theological concerns, it must be *all* the concerns of *all* the theologians. Once again we can succumb to the temptation to limit or select what we would like to hear. We mentioned just above in our treatment of Wisdom that not too long ago it was unfashionable to include Wisdom material in such a summary of Old Testament theology because, in the view of the great Gerhard Von Rad, it was "slightly tinged with the pallor of theological reflection." It did not adequately attend to Israel's historical traditions that for these scholars were the heart of the Old Testament. A pessimist like Qoheleth or even Job sitting among the ashes had nothing worthwhile to contribute. This was, of course, a classic case of selecting a canon within the canon—whereas our canon has to be *all* the Scriptures Jesus knew, whether tradition critics of yesteryear warm to them or not. So the scope of Old Testament theology has to be all those theologians in Israel—not forgetting the context provided by contemporary extrabiblical theologians or at least composers who influenced them. The theology of *Job* takes on added meaning if we know the Babylonian Theodicy (which you'll find in *ANET*).

The Word speaks to us

Ideally, we should listen to these ancient theologians as believers and theologians ourselves: what they have to say influences our faith and theologizing, as Calvin so eloquently put it above. It is possible to stand back and clinically examine and describe how they came to gradually clearer insight into God and God's plan for Israel, how Qoheleth endeavored to refine a pat scheme of reward and punishment trotted out by the proverb makers. In that process, however, we may fail to respect the purpose of the Word, to achieve a meeting also with us: the Word speaks to us surely. When we read *Joel* in our Lenten liturgies, it is not simply to determine what he meant to a lax community of his time, but to apply his message to us in our situation, the possibility that "the day of the Lord is near, and as destruction from the Almighty it comes" (1.15). The Old Testament Word is not a dead text for a lost community but a living voice for ours.

So, when we do listen to all those theologians speaking to their community and to us, what do we hear? We hear a series of recurring concerns, or theological themes, such as we have studied one by one in this text: election, deliverance, wilderness experience, covenant relationship, the Land, sin and repentance, suffering and evil, and many others. We find them whether we study the text in its gradual development or in the final canonical form that has come down to us.

Is there any overriding theme that gives unity to the variety of concerns? Many recent commentators have looked for such a "center" of Old Testament theology, an organizing principle that could be said to perform that function for us in our Western quest for system. Walter Eichrodt and others found it in the covenant of Yahweh with Israel, Walther Zimmerli in the name of God, Samuel Terrien in divine presence, Claus Westermann in salvation and blessing, others in the Holy, in kingdom, and so on. At least these are Old Testament concerns, not the categories of Western theology, but they are generally inadequate to gather in the theologizing of all those ancient thinkers.

A central message

Perhaps we can settle for a central message of the Old Testament in a comprehensive formula such as "God's care for a people of his choice"; that is certainly a presupposition of all the composers. From his vantage point of the time after Jesus, Paul the Jew would interpret it all as "the mystery of Christ"—as we saw in ch. 14—but it is not a phrase those authors would have used. Jesus, we saw, did expect his contemporaries to have achieved such a meaningful interpretation of "Moses", of "the Law and the Prophets", and even lectured some groups on finding it. As members of the community of his followers we should with his guidance be able to unlock the theological riches of the Scriptures he knew.

Further reading

G. W. Coates, "Theology of the Hebrew Bible," *The Hebrew Bible and its Modern Interpreters*, 239–62

R. C. Dentan, *Preface to Old Testament Theology*, rev. edn, New York: Seabury, 1963

K. Stendahl, "Contemporary biblical theology," *IDB* I, 418–32

B. S. Childs, *Biblical Theology in Crisis*, Philadelphia: Westminster, 1970

J. Barr, "Biblical theology," *IDB Supp* 104–111

S. Terrien, "Biblical theology: the Old Testament (1970–84). A decade and a half of spectacular growth," *BTB* 15 (1985 No. 4) 127–35

GLOSSARY

If a word you are seeking does not appear, look for it in the General
Index.

APOCALYPTIC literature endeavors to provide special access to revelation
(Greek *apocalypsis*) through a series of visions, dreams, exotic imagery
dealing especially with Israel's and the world's end (see ch. 11).

APOCRYPHA (Greek 'hidden, obscure') is the name given (by Protestants)
to books thought undeserving of a place in the Bible (e.g. *Tobit,
Maccabees*). Catholics and Orthdox, who include these books and speak
of them as deuterocanonical, use "apocryphal" to refer to other books
from Old Testament times found in no Christian Bibles, e.g. *Enoch* (see
ch. 3).

CANON, a Greek word for "rule, yardstick", refers to the collection of
a community's scriptures that has been authoritatively judged on various
criteria to be canonical or normative for that community (see ch. 3).

CANONICAL CRITICISM requires the student to find the meaning of
an (Old Testament) text not in isolation but within the whole canon
of which it is a part (see ch. 14).

COVENANT, or treaty or alliance (*testamentum* in Latin), is the word used
in the Bible as a political figure for the relationship God forms with
his people (as on Sinai) or with individuals like Noah and Abraham.

CRITICISM, from the Greek for "judge, evaluate", means, in biblical and
general literary matters, evaluation of a piece of literature; so there is
nothing negative about critical techniques (unlike English use of
"critical" in other contexts), of which there are various kinds (see chs
4 and 14).

DECALOGUE, lit. "ten words" in Greek, refers to that part of the
covenant formula in *Exodus* and *Deuteronomy* that we call Ten Commandments.

DEUTEROCANONICAL (see CANON) refers to those Old Testament
books admitted to the canon (of Catholics and Orthodox), though thus

217

in a second (Greek *deuteros*) category by comparison with Protocanonical books.

ESCHATOLOGICAL, an adjective from Greek *eschaton*, "last things, end, goal", has the sense of looking towards or moving to the goal instead of remaining static.

EXEGESIS, a Greek term for "explanation," is applied to the work of EXEGETES in explaining the sense of biblical texts through textual, linguistic, literary and historical examination.

The FATHERS of the (Christian) Church, great spokesmen, theologians, bishops and catechists of the six or seven centuries after the compilation of the New Testament (like Origen and Chrysostom in the East, Augustine and Jerome), left us commentaries on the books of Old and New Testaments.

FUNDAMENTALISM is the opposite of criticism; evaluative techniques are avoided and a simplistic approach adopted to texts that in fact require solid study for proper understanding, such as creation stories, apocalyptic material; see ch. 11.

HELLENISTIC, from the Greek word for "Greek," refers to the period and culture when Greek influence held sway in the biblical world.

HERMENEUTICS is the study of meaning and the ways to interpret biblical texts (see chs 10 & 14).

HYPOSTATIZATION means the elevation of a virtue or characteristic, such as wisdom, to the status of a person (Greek *hypostasis*), as happens in some of the Wisdom books of the Old Testament.

INCARNATIONAL theology stresses God's sacramental way of dealing with us so that spiritual goods come to us through tangible realities, such as the words and events of salvation history.

INERRANCY means freedom from error in biblical texts, and is one (if not the principal) effect of their being inspired by God (see ch. 8).

LEVITES, as their name suggests, were members of the tribe of Levi. Though not automatically priests (who were supposed to be descendants of Aaron within that tribe), there were periods when Levites alone acted as priests, and at other times they discharged lesser tasks in worship.

LXX, Latin numeral for "seventy," *septuaginta*, is used to indicate the Greek version of the Old Testament, the Septuagint, made over the last few centuries before Jesus, which legend says was the work of seventy or so scholars who produced identical versions.

The MASORETIC text (MT) of the Hebrew Bible, which is a well-preserved medieval form giving us our best manuscripts, comes from Jewish scholars, or masoretes (Hebrew *massoret*, "tradition"), from Babylon and Palestine; this form of the text, though late, includes vowels and is thus easier to read.

MESSIAH is the English form of Aramaic and Hebrew words for "anointed," which in Greek is *christos*—whether one of a series of messiahs, salvific figures, or *the* Messiah, that anointed king of David's line who would bring the world under God's reign (see ch. 13).

MIDRASH, from Hebrew *darash*, "investigate," is the type of commentary on biblical texts that comes to us from the rabbis (see Appendix 2).

The MISHNAH (Hebrew for "study, repetition") is the codification of rabbinic laws, or "oral Torah," applying the written Torah to all aspects of life. With further bodies of rabbinic commentary it forms the Talmud (see Appendix 2).

MOSAIC Law, for example, is the law that Moses conveyed to the people of Israel after receiving it from Yahweh on Sinai.

MYTH, in theological language, is a figurative overlay applied to persons or events in an effort to make their significance clearer. The term does not, therefore, denote falsity or fiction, though a myth may be stronger on truth than on fact.

NEW CRITICISM switches the focus of attention in biblical study from the author to the work (see ch. 14).

PASCHAL is the adjective from Hebrew *pesach*, Passover.

PERICOPE is a word used of a clearly delineated passage of Scripture taken for study, like one prophetic oracle or a brief incident.

PHARISEES, whose name means "set apart," were a lay group that arose in the Hellenistic period (as opposed to the priestly group the Sadducees, tracing their name from Zadok the priest) distinguished by their respect for the oral Torah, which they considered "a fence around the Law." The New Testament, with its own axe to grind, does not credit them with such flexibility.

PSEUDEPIGRAPHICAL (or pseudonymous) works are those that bear the name of composers not in fact responsible for them, like Wisdom books attributed to Solomon—or similar intertestamental books, which Protestants call Pseudepigrapha, and others call Apocrypha.

RABBI, "my great one," is a term not generally used until New Testament times, but this class of Jewish commentator and teacher arose in Old Testament times, producing oral Torah and the *midrashim* (see Appendix 2).

REDACTION is the word used for incorporation of previously existing source material into a meaningful literary and theological whole. Redactors could thus be skilful artists and theologians (see ch. 14).

SITZ IM LEBEN (German for "place in the life") is a term used when we are looking for the real-life situation from which a biblical pericope came, such as a psalm or collection of proverbs, before finding its way into the text.

SAPIENTIAL is the adjective for the Wisdom (Latin *sapientia*) books of the Old (and New) Testament.

STRUCTURALISM is that approach to the Old (and New) Testament that studies patterns in the text (see ch. 14).

TALMUD: see MISHNAH.

TESTAMENT: see COVENANT and Appendix 1, "What's in a name?"

General Index

Index of biblical citations

Index of modern authors